JOHN H. NOTA, S.J.

Phenomenology and History

Translated by Louis Grooten and the author

LOYOLA UNIVERSITY PRESS

Chicago, Illinois

1967

© 1967 Loyola University Press
Printed in the United States of America
Library of Congress Catalog Card Number: 67-13891

PREFACE

This book had its origin in the existential need of a historian to tell himself and others just what *history* means. What began as a short introduction to the philosophy of history grew slowly into a book. I am happy to have had the opportunity to check my opinions with others during lectures at the Berchmanianum, the Jesuit Faculty of Philosophy in Nijmegen, at Duquesne University, Pittsburgh, at Loyola University, Chicago, at the University of San Francisco, and at many other places in Europe and the United States. I wish to thank the philosophers, theologians, historians, and especially the many students, who all have taught me by their critical observations and questions.

I am glad to be able to make use of some criticisms of the original Dutch edition. They have helped me adapt this English version to its different circumstances and to the always-dynamic truth. It is impossible to mention all who have helped me with this edition, but I should like particularly to thank Miss Margaret Vojtko, at the University of Pittsburgh, for her never-failing accuracy. Dr. Louis Grooten, a man of many talents, spent painstaking years on the translation, with ready assistance from Father Tom O'Malley, S.J. Father Ted Tracy's knowledge of Greek was invaluable, and Father Torrens Hecht, S.J., assured the finishing touches.

JOHN H. NOTA, S.J.

Berchmanianum
Nijmegen, The Netherlands

CONTENTS

THE STARTING POINT

OF THE

PHILOSOPHY OF HISTORY

The professional historian eyes the philosophy of history askance—and even those who do not share his aversion can understand it—for the subject as he sees it is a kind of dictatorship by philosophers who think that they can settle a priori, deductively, what history ought to be. Their starting point is the ivory-tower attitude of their own philosophy, which pays not the slightest heed to historiography as a discipline or to that realm of the past which is home to the historian. And so he will seem to hear a language from another world, a discussion about things unknown to him, when philosophers presume to speak about the nature of history, a subject which is not unfamiliar to him, after all, since he has studied it devotedly for years. If the method of the philosophy of history is like that, the historian has no use for it, and irritated, he rejects all philosophy of history completely.

The question arises whether irritation has served the historian well or whether his studies would not have benefited more from greater forbearance. One may, in fact, ask if there might not be another philosophy of history, one with a different starting point, which would take into account the factualness of things. If so, it will no longer be necessary for the historian to turn away. Instead he will opt for an encounter between the discipline of history and the philosophy of history, to their common advantage. I intend to show that there is nothing strained in such an encounter but, on the contrary, that historical praxis itself demonstrates the necessity for a philosophy of history, while the latter should start from actual historical praxis to discover from its factualness the essence of history.

To be quite fair, I must mention that Johan Huizinga, the famous Dutch historian, used to warn those of his inquiring students who wondered what history really was not to give the matter a great deal of thought. "I used to tell my students who often revealed an inclination toward the theory of history: 'Make yourselves acquainted with it, but do not burrow too deep for it will turn your mind from the historian's real work'" (author's translation).[1]

From a teacher's point of view Huizinga was right. For the young student of history the practical answer to this question lies in the study of history itself. This will occupy him, and it is by actually pursuing the discipline that the first practical answer to his question will be brought home to him. Movement is best demonstrated by moving.

But that is not the end of the matter. This first answer cannot be the final one or the most profound. The question will arise spontaneously and recurrently, especially in the practical study

2

of history. In fact, Huizinga himself provided a detailed theoretical answer in "Cultuurhistorische verkenningen" (Explorations of Cultural History) and "De wetenschap der geschiedenis" (The Discipline of History).[2] For the man who reflects, practice of itself requires a theory to support it. And this introduces another point.

The need for a philosophy of history as revealed by the praxis of history

The practical study of history is in danger of getting into a blind alley. Ortega y Gasset has shown that there is strong dissatisfaction with the discipline of history in its entire range because it is bogged down in paltry facts dug from archives by grubbers in documents. Thus, it fails to come within the scope of historical science, which is supposed to be a reconstruction of facts.[3] It is true that Ortega's pronouncement may have been made in whimsical spirit, that it is an oversimplification which does not discriminate sufficiently among the various legitimate ways of scholarly praxis. Nevertheless, the late Jan Romein, a well-known Dutch historian, had arrived at the same conclusion when he put it bluntly: specialization is causing the study of history to run aground and is raising a serious barrier to the advancement of historiography.[4] And G. J. Renier of London has said, "If professional historians refuse to write general history, their duty will be carried out by amateurs."[5]

If, then, the practice of historical studies no longer has a practical answer even to the question of what it ought to be because this very practice is in danger of going wrong, the historian will find himself compelled to look for help elsewhere, from outside the province of history. So history points to the necessity for a "meta-history" (a term coined by Ortega y Gasset on the analogy of *metaphysics*), which is going to tell us what history essentially is.[6] This does not mean, though, that we have already arrived at the philosophy of history in the strict

3

sense, for not every reflection by the historian on his profession must needs be a philosophical one. But this is what such reflection should result in, and not until it does will it be complete, according to Marc Bloch. There is doubtless room, however, for a theory of history, a methodology, an exposition of its professional technique, such as has been excellently provided by Bloch himself.[7]

Thus, in our search for the nature of history we must pass through several phases. To begin with, there is the praxis of historical studies with its practical answer. Next, because this actual practice is in danger of becoming no longer adequate, comes theoretical history. Finally, as a complement to the theory, which too is insufficient alone, follows the philosophy of history. The need for this third phase is best demonstrated by the ideas about theoretical history which Romein advocated. Greatly concerned about the deadlock in which the study of history found itself as a result of overspecialization, Romein attempted to solve the problem by introducing a new academic subject, of which he was the first to take the chair in the Amsterdam Municipal University. He gave it the name "theoretical history." His solution has also become known outside the Netherlands and has given rise to frequent debates. Certainly it merits further discussion here. I shall therefore give Romein's views first and then my own opinion of them. In this way, I hope, the necessity for a philosophy of history will become clearer to the reader.

In a lecture delivered at Groningen in 1946, entitled "Theoretische geschiedenis"—it also appeared in an English translation, "Theoretical History," and in German—Romein gave a brief and lucid exposition of his views. In later publications he repeatedly returned to this subject, at greatest length in his book *In de hof der historie* (In the Garden of History).[8]

Theoretical history, Romein tells us, is a new and comprehensive subject. It is a reflection upon "history as a discipline" and "history as a happening." It is to practical history what

4

theoretical physics is to applied physics. Theoretical history is the knowledge of what history is, practical history the knowledge of what has happened. Theoretical history is distinguished from practical history—which, as we saw before, is in danger of running aground through overspecialization—by its theoretical approach. It differs from the philosophy of history, which theorizes about history without actually knowing it, in its starting point; that is, the actual pursuit of history. Accordingly, as an object of study the theory of history covers the entire territory between the somewhat naïve praxis of history and the philosophy of history, which latter tends to divorce itself from the history pursued by working historians. Theoretical history, as a reflection of the historian's activities, comprises—Romein does not pretend completeness here—the following five provinces:

> the first . . . purely theoretical problems and problems of method; the second, the study of the pattern and rhythm of history; the third, the breakdown of the past into periods, and recognition of the driving powers in history; the fourth, a number of topics dealing with the past, which nevertheless cannot by their nature be considered "ordinary" historiography; and the fifth, the study of historiography.[9]

So much for Romein's view. If it should appear a little vague, the originator of the system claims our indulgence in advance because a novel discipline is bound to be lacking in strict form and completeness. It would be ungrateful not to bear in mind the difficulties encountered by Romein in his pioneer work, and we do owe him a debt of recognition. His was a signal contribution to the study of history, though I cannot fully agree with him.

In voicing my opinion of Romein's views here, I must begin by stressing the importance of the fact that by developing his "theoretical history" Romein made the first important move to free history from its contemporary deadlock, looking as he did for a solution to the difficulties outside the current praxis of history. To be sure, it was this actual practice which forced him to do so because even that practice could no longer supply him with a practical answer; but whereas others evaded the issue, Romein tackled it. The question What is history? is one that transcends history proper and therefore must receive its answer from a new discipline, theoretical history. Now the problem is how far Romein's solution will take us toward the real solution. Can theoretical history, as interpreted by him, provide us with the correct answer to that meta-historical question? Is this theory of any help to the historian in his everyday work?

Reluctantly I must say that in my opinion Romein has not wholly achieved his aims. Theoretical history as seen by him is only quantitatively, and not essentially, different from practical history and, for this reason, is not exempt from the difficulties that beset the practical study of history. Consequently, theoretical history will not be able to answer the meta-historical question put to it.

No doubt it is of great use—above all, paradoxically enough, in the practical pursuit of historical studies—but it does not supply us with a universal remedy. Once we are engaged in the study of theoretical history, the need for a meta-historical philosophy of history becomes even more evident.

Let me try to make this clear from Romein's argument.

As has been seen, theoretical history comprises various areas. One of them is historiography, the study of historical studies. It is apparent that such a return to the past has its uses; it provides us with numerous practical answers to our question, voiced by many students of history. One may go even further, as Fritz Wagner did in an excellent work which has for its theme the origins of the study of history and what the subject tells us about its own nature.[10]

Thus we arrive at a history of the study of history, no doubt instructive in both theoretical and practical aspects but always having the inevitable drawback: all these factual considerations can never give us more than a factual result—telling us what has happened—perhaps with the negative conclusion that certain ways of studying history, such as our present-day specialization, cannot hold their own in actual practice. But this is not yet that kind of reflection on what the historian is doing which essentially transcends history. Historical things, as well as historical thinking, are still an intrinsic part of theoretical history. It is true that the sort of history which can be termed "theoretical," because of its differently orientated sequence or for other reasons, has a claim to a special title; but such differences remain ones of degree only. Despite my theoretical point of view, my concern at this moment is still with the praxis of history; and consequently I am left at a loss by the difficulties it presents, which are still those that theoretical history is eager to surmount. Romein is aware of this problem when, in his introduction to J. van der Pot's work on periodization, he defends the author against the stricture that he is silent about the underlying causes of the phenomenon, by saying that it is a problem which lies outside the order of periods presented in the work.[11] But this "beyond," according to Romein, remains part of theoretical history, whose tasks involve solving in a historical way—that is, by means of a theory arrived at by an "adstruction of facts"—such supra-historical questions as the objectivity of history, historical causality, historical judgment, and the nature of history.[12] Thus Romein responds to the inquiry into the nature of history through ten examples from history.[13] Highly illustrative, very useful indeed, is his view; but it serves as reply only to the question of what people's ideas about the nature of history have been in the course of time, not to the real question of what history is.

Evidence based on historical facts, however skillfully compiled, will never provide more than historical certainty. But the supra-historical questions reaching us from throughout history demand a supra-historical reply. This, however, will carry us into the field of meta-history, which essentially transcends theoretical history because the latter is only partially capable of responding to the questions put to it by history. Just as the praxis of history points to its theory, as Romein shows us, so theoretical history points to the philosophy of history. It is only there that supra-historical questions—which, although transcending historical factualness, Romein would leave to a special branch of theoretical history—can possibly receive their supra-historical answers.

Such questions are not to be referred to philosophy, however, as to some *deus ex machina* which comes miraculously to history's assistance when history cannot help itself either practically or theoretically. Philosophy has been implicit in both practical and theoretical history all the time. The historian must of necessity work with certain viewpoints on history, man, truth, objectivity, and other subjects. In other words, he has a built-in a priori to guide his thoughts on history. This generally accepted concept is formulated in Romein's paradox that "a historian's value lies primarily in what he knows about man, rather than in what he knows about the past."[14] His Marxist views testified to this. But if such an a priori will guide the historian's whole way of thinking, it is at once immanent and transcendent, so that its ultimate motivations are not to be found in history alone but must be attributed to a way of thinking which, while standing in an essential relationship to history, at the same time transcends it. And it is this that we seek in the philosophy of history.

The philosophy of history

The need for a philosophy of history has been established by starting from the praxis of historical studies. Such a philosophy is implicit in history itself, which is why for the starting point of its explicitation we will again have to turn to historical praxis. On the one hand, therefore, we can do nothing with a

8

philosophy of history which proceeds in a purely a priori manner, disregards historical facts, and is an offense to historians. In this respect I fully agree with Romein and many others. Such a philosophy of history would be merely transcendent, quite above the level of history and devoid of contact with it. Hence it would be different from the implicit philosophy already found and whose explicitation we are seeking. That kind of philosophy would not pertain to history's a priori because this is immanent as well as transcendent.

On the other hand, we must not be tempted to adopt the position of the opposite extreme and accept a philosophy of history which, bogged down in relativism, fails to transcend. Of this, R. Aron's *Introduction à la philosophie de l'histoire* is an example.[15] Aron has written an excellent work; but because of his rejection of the absolute, his philosophy remains purely relativistic, essentially and intrinsically bound up with time. As a result, it is absorbed by history. In the fields of the transcendent and supra-historical, which are the very reasons for its existence, it fails by remaining purely immanent, though at a high level. In the same way, Romein remains a relativist when out of sheer necessity he assigns a place to philosophy in determining the meaning of history. In fact, a real philosophy of history must satisfy two demands: it must transcend history and at the same time must be intrinsic to it. It will start from the praxis of history, from contact with historical factualness, but when in a phenomenological analysis of historical praxis (in which it must rely greatly on theoretical history) the philosophy of history is attempting to "get at" the nature of history, it is faced by a different factualness, that of the supra-historical a priori, which is immanent as well as transcendent to history. Philosophy discovers itself in the factualness of the human mind. In the explicitation of the implicit philosophy offered us by this a priori, by this mind, we arrive at a certainty that is of a nature different from the historical one precisely because it explicitates the supra-historical moment, thereby surpassing time and thus being absolute. The negation of the truths found here would not be a negation of some particular fact but the negation of the factualness of the mind itself; that is, in our negation an affirmation is implied. True, we have arrived at this philosophical certainty of what history is, guided by historical factualness, but the certainty does not derive from that factualness. "In experience, not from experience," phenomenology teaches us.

Such a philosophy of history must not lose itself in historical factualness but must remain concrete because it is always recovering itself in this factualness. The deadlock of pure, timeless abstraction and the pure temporality of concreteness can be solved, I think, by a philosophy of history which, as philosophy, rises above history while always presupposing its presence, thereby remaining essentially—yet extrinsically—dependent upon it. Therefore, the starting point of the philosophy of history is the praxis of historical studies subject to the proviso that it be seen in its completeness; that is, inclusive of the realization in time of the human mind's a priori.

SPECIFYING OUR STARTING POINT

The starting point of the philosophy of history, as I understand it, is in historical studies, the discipline of history. History is "a discipline in its infancy," in Bloch's words.[1] This is why even Romein cannot give offhand a definitive exposition of theoretical history. There is yet no long tradition of reflection on the historian's work because the scholarly approach to his studies began relatively recently.

Nowadays some people are censuring St. Thomas Aquinas for not having left a philosophy of history, but such strictures demonstrate a considerable lack of historical sense. Aquinas did not write a meta-history because history as such, as we know it, simply did not exist in the thirteenth century. We might as well blame him for not giving us in his *Summa* a clear opinion on the morality of the atomic bomb. On the other hand, we do find in his works the principles underlying a philosophy of history, for medieval man was fully aware of his historical roots. I shall have occasion to consider this matter later on.

If we are apt to stress the fact that not until the nineteenth century did the discipline of history come truly into its own, this does not mean that man has not reflected upon his past until recent times. The facts tell a different story. To some extent man has always been interested in his past, and we may find proof of this in ancient documents—drawn, carved, written—and in the sagas and myths of glorious deeds which were told and sung by wandering bards, some of which (like Homer's *Iliad* and *Odyssey*) we still enjoy.

A new genre was introduced in the writings of the man whom Cicero called "the father of history," Herodotus (484-425 B.C.). To be sure, the tales of the past had been handed down before his time, but in his era the first truly critical historiography was realized in Greece. A new point can be made here: the discipline of history, historiography, has its own history, too. From it we learn how Herodotus' descendants, although not exactly unworthy of their ancestor, in later times came to conduct themselves in a manner he would never have approved of. Though Huizinga was justified in criticizing the historiographical classification of the German historian Ernst Bernheim (1850-1942), I believe that in a slightly modified form it may still be useful as a brief outline of the history of historiography.[2]

Herodotus is the characteristic representative of those historiographers whose only wish is to narrate, passing from one story to the next. Sometimes they tell their tales with great skill, in a fine style. Bernheim calls this method *das referierende Erzählen* ("reporting narrative").

12

Side by side with this approach, rather than as a later phase, pragmatic or didactic history evolved; that is, the attempt to give the facts insofar as they convey some idea or teach something, in order that history may be, in Cicero's words, *magistra vitae*, "life's teacher." Examples of this method are presented by Thucydides (455-396 B.C.), Tacitus (A.D. 55-120), St. Augustine (354-430), Macchiavelli (1469-1529), Bossuet (1627-1704), Hegel (1770-1831), and George Bancroft (1800-1891). What I consider pragmatic history may be exemplified by an opinion on Bancroft's *History of the United States* which said that "every volume voted for Jackson."[3]

True, in our days too one will find aspects of these two kinds of historiography—obvious examples are the Marxist and the Fascist conceptions of history—but nevertheless since the nineteenth century we have become aware of a new element in the pursuit of history which transforms it into an academic discipline and, to quote Lousse, "removes history from the temple of the Muses, where she was worshipped as Clio, to a university seminar in the German tradition, and to the dust-covered tables of scholarship."[4]

This move was not an unexpected one, however; for some time there had been a growth toward the transition. Although, generally speaking, in the days of Humanism and the Renaissance men lacked a sense of history—as we may see from the disdain in which they held their immediate predecessors and, in fact, almost any era except that of antiquity and their own—at any rate their critical sense sharpened. Thus Lorenzo Valla (1405-1457) discovered the falsifications of the Pseudo-Dionysius; the Bollandists set themselves the task of raising the critical standards of hagiography. A true pioneer who understood that things historical had a character of their own was the Italian philosopher Giovanni Battista Vico (1668-1744). He explicitly distinguished history, as a study of human things, from the natural sciences. But Vico, a veritably great thinker, was far ahead of his contemporaries; and after a century, in Germany, Johann Gottfried von Herder (1744-1803) had to make another start, this time with greater success. The French Revolution and the Napoleonic era, finally, taught Europe that previous periods were not simply worthless. So it was that in the nineteenth century romanticism and a severely academic approach combined in a curious way to arrive at the "genetic conception of history." "Genetic historiography traces the uninterrupted development of some event or situation from innumerable internal and external processes. The genetic historian wishes to know how every historical phenomenon has come to be what it is, how it has evolved from the texture of existing facts" (author's translation).[5]

In the next period history became a genuinely academic discipline, so that a theory, a philosophy, could be devised to assign history its proper place in the realm of learning. The great pioneers of human studies (*Geisteswissenschaften*) were Wilhelm Dilthey (1833-1911), a German, and his fellow countrymen the neo-Kantian philosophers Windelband (1848-1915) and Rickert (1863-1936).[6] Their philosophy was to be of great value to the study of history itself. In fact, the genetic method offers a number of further possibilities.

Finally, in our own day, we see a trend toward "synthetic historiography," as a reaction to overspecialization. Toynbee's writings may be considered a specimen of this description of history or some of its periods by one or more historians in such a manner that each detail remains subordinated to the whole.

The discipline of history has seen many branches of specialization sprout from its tree, especially since its coming of age in the nineteenth century. We have been presented with histories of states, nations, mankind, culture, and art. Huizinga pleaded for a history of the garden, the road, the marketplace, the inn, and three creatures which played a role in civilization—the horse, the dog, and the falcon. He also appealed for

14

a history of the functions of the hat and the book in society.[7] Frederick van der Meer gave us in his fine *Geschiedenis van een kathedraal* the history of a French cathedral.[8] Geologists, stretching the use of the word, even talk about the history of the earth's crust. No doubt we shall have to take account of the multiform use of the term *history* if we wish to keep to our starting point, the praxis of historical study. In doing so, however, we run the risk of losing our bearings among the diversity of forms and of not getting beyond our complex starting point. It would seem, though, that this danger can be avoided by reflecting on this factualness. The discipline of history will then be seen to be primarily that branch of learning which deals with man in the past. The history of animals or dead matter not directly related to man is, as such, merely of secondary importance. When speaking about history we refer not to the "history" of the earth's crust but to one of the numerous forms of human history. This fact will be my starting point for the moment. At a later stage in my argument I shall have to justify my stand and substantiate my classification of the various kinds of history. Here I am concerned only with the history of man in its present phase.

A phenomenological view

Our philosophical aim is to discover from the historian's practical experience what history is. Accordingly, the starting point of this phenomenological philosophy of history must be the praxis of historical studies. How does the historian pursue this discipline?

Let us assume that I, a student of the history of philosophy, wish to investigate the philosophical-theological instruction of the Dominicans during the first fifty years of the order's existence (1208-1258). What am I doing in occupying myself with this theme? I am turning around to look at the past.

I must confess that I have used the term *the past* somewhat rashly. As a rule its significance is not appreciated. As we reflect upon it we shall find that, properly speaking, the past does not exist for the historian. To him it is an amorphous mass: a mere accumulation of inscriptions, documents, and facts, having no order or significance.[9]

But my look at the past does not take place by chance. I can speak about it only insofar as I, a human being, ask questions of this chaos and only insofar as I consider some part of the welter of data a unified whole—in this instance bounded by the years 1208, when St. Dominic founded his order, and 1258, when St. Thomas was *magister theologiae* at the University of Paris. Not only does this period mean a specific span of years for me; from the many happenings of those years I single out one aspect only: the evolution of philosophical-theological instruction in the Dominican order during that time. Other events —the foundation of the order itself, its approbation by Pope Honorius III in 1216, religious life in the thirteenth century, the contemporaneous vocation of St. Francis of Assisi and his ideals, the attitude of Pope Innocent III, the deeds of Frederick II in Italy and Germany, those of St. Louis in France, the translations of Aristotle and the commentaries upon his writings, the regulations issued by the University of Paris against him—are only discussed in order to throw light upon the main topic of investigation; they find their proper place and function in subordination to the framework of the whole.

Were another historian to describe the development of Franciscan instruction during the same period, that subject would dominate and Dominican instruction would be relegated to a minor position even if in a wider context its importance for the history of philosophy and theology were more fundamental. The historian, whether his concern be with the Crusades or the conquests of Genghis Khan (1167-1227), will always, by the very fact of his research, find himself confronted with a particular entity—the life of some person, the vicissitudes of a community, the fluctuations in a cultural phenomenon such as the

16

higher studies of the Black Friars—a whole, limited by time and space, in which he observes a series of changes.

Such a whole may be assigned various names, each of which shapes it into another unit. Voltaire derided the time-honored division of history according to the reigns of monarchs: "It would seem that for fourteen centuries no other people have lived in Gaul than kings, ministers of the Crown, and generals" (author's translation).[10] Later on, civilization received its due. Historians spoke of the Renaissance, capitalizing the period; and offering a semblance of practicality and neutrality, they categorized the past by centuries.

In the instance, especially, of writing a history of some particular century the caesura is highly artificial indeed. It is common for historians to begin such a history by correcting a misconception. They may say, for example, that "their" century begins at an earlier date or ends later than is usually supposed. Thus Charles H. Haskins in the first chapter of *The Renaissance of the Twelfth Century* informs us that the high tide of the civilization he will discuss has its proper beginning around 1050 and that the great work of renewal is completed circa 1250: "Chronological limits are not easy to set. Centuries are at best but arbitrary conveniences which must not be permitted to clog or to distort our historical thinking: history cannot remain history if sawed off into even lengths of hundreds of years."[11] Common sense tells us that there is no law about decisive events' occurring at the turn of each century. This is why the "millenarist" movement is obviously based on irrational factors. All the same, such a division of historical time into centuries does have its advantages, the more so as it helps us to realize time's relativity.[12]

Be that as it may, one of the first facts which we encounter when analyzing the practice of historical studies is that by the very fact of our investigation we become confronted with a whole, a unit, which on the one hand is dependent upon our investigation—on our quest and the quests of other scholars—

17

but which on the other hand is independent of them. My question is essential if I am to hear the voice of the past, but I can do no more than record its response. The answer must not be manipulated in any way. The entity discovered by my quest has a life of its own. It will change, develop, languish—it may even die—and be absorbed into a higher entity. This happens in all historical research, even if we are investigating the history of mankind. The object by which I am confronted is always a unit. Its frontiers may be very vague—"from the beginnings of mankind to our days"—but the object always presents the same characteristics. It is a whole, subject to change; it is in progress a happening.

The first conclusion has been reached: history as a science is inseparably linked with a whole which, too, we designate by the name *history*, history as a happening. A given book deals, let us say, with the history of the United States. Our present analysis has its starting point in the history of the Dominicans' philosophical-theological instruction during the first decades of their order. It is with this kind of history—that is, history as a happening—that our branch of learning is concerned. To be sure, the word *history* has many other meanings. It goes back to the Greek ἱστορία, which originally stood for "investigation" in general; this is the meaning in which the word is used by Aristotle (we still have the term *natural history*).[13] But adhering to our starting point, the praxis of historical studies, we find the same word used to indicate two diverse realities: history as a discipline, as a science, and history as a happening (*histoire science—histoire réalité*).

I shall deal in this order with these two realities, but first I wish to stress, beyond their difference, their unity and interrelationship. History as a science presupposes history as a happening. Heidegger has given a good deal of thought to this in *Sein und Zeit*. His uncompromising view is that the existential interpretation of history as a science aims only at the verifica-

18

tion of its ontological origin from the historicity of *Dasein* ("being there").[14] Such radicalism is the more striking when we consider that Heidegger refuses to acknowledge historical science as a starting point for the solution of the problem of history because, according to him, such an approach would prevent us from penetrating sufficiently into the essence of history, since the very object of our historical science would bog us down.[15]

Doubtless Heidegger is right in pointing to the origin of historical science from history as a happening. To put it more concisely: it is because man *is* history that we have history. I shall consider this ontological structure of man as a historical being in detail in the next section. By then it will be clear that Heidegger's unilateral relation ought rather to be a mutual one, that history as a science and history as a happening presuppose each other. Our starting point, the fact of historical science, is no obstacle on our path toward the essence of history. Indeed, it helps us to find the right way.

The interrelation, then, between history as a science and history as a happening may provisionally be summed up in the following way:

First, we have already seen in our phenomenological analysis that on one hand history as a happening is discovered by man's reflecting on his past and thus being faced by an ever-varying unity; and on the other hand, this reflection on the past is only feasible because the past does exist.

Second, history as a science, taken alone, is likewise a happening. I have mentioned the history of historiography (Stern, Wagner, Fueter), in which history has itself as object.

Third, to a certain extent history as a happening is identical with history as a science because in this human happening a reflection on the past, implying science, must somehow be present. If we take this view, we shall not stop short at the object of historical science in a strict sense. With Heidegger we shall reject such an attitude as not sufficiently profound and instead attempt

19

to arrive, this time by way of historical science, at the "historicity of *Dasein*" itself. In this *Dasein* we discover how it derives its "being history" from the self-reflection which links past, present, and future, and hence is capable of bestowing upon the past a unity which it by itself is lacking. What explicit historical science did for its object is done here by self-reflection, the implicit historical science embodied in *Dasein*. And in this case too, it must be clear that history as a happening and history as a science (explicit or implicit) presuppose each other.

So far for the moment. It seemed important to begin by emphasizing the unity of these two aspects of history before considering them individually. In this way an understanding of their unity may better be acquired in the next section.

III

HISTORY AS A HAPPENING—

THE MEANING OF HISTORY

The question What is history? hardly troubles the layman. He considers it academic, and therefore it is of little interest to him so long as it refers explicitly to history as a branch of learning. Its distinctions do not touch him, so he remains indifferent to them until he becomes aware that in history as a discipline is contained another history, history as a happening. This second aspect of the subject does concern him; it affects his interests, his person, his family, his life.

Two world wars within thirty years, with a "cold war" following in their wake and the threat of another, incomparably more terrible, lowering over our lives at this time, have brought home the importance of this issue to modern man in all strata of society and throughout the world. In the past, insecurity was the fate of a single social group, the working class; and in one continent alone did they try to free themselves from that predicament. Nowadays social and national consciousness has grown stronger everywhere, but curiously enough, it has been attended by general insecurity. It is no longer possible for the citizen in Europe to lead the quiet life his father did—providing for himself and his family, striving after greater prosperity and firmly convinced that it will one day be his, assured by prudent saving of a comfortable old age, perhaps not overanxious about other people or nations not so blessed with worldly goods. Of course, this attitude still exists in some individuals and in some areas, but actually those in whom it is found live outside their time, divorced from reality. Even a maximum number of insurance premiums cannot camouflage the fact that our lives have been deprived of a fundamental security. Man has sustained a shock to his mundane existence. He spends his days worrying about the present and the future; he has seen the illusion of progress exploded; he is forced to play a part in a worldwide drama in which he and his fellow beings appear to be mere puppets.

He continues to perform his daily work, but he has misgivings about its purpose and wonders whether in the crazy era of the H-bomb there is any worth in life. His bewilderment widens into a questioning of the significance of the civilization he is called upon to defend as his heritage and of all the seemingly senseless events taking place around him. This problem— vaguely understood by many and defiantly answered by modern youth's terse So what?—is simply the popular expression of the question What is history?

The actual state of the question

The present interest in this question accounts for a good many recent answers. Before 1920 the publications which concerned themselves with the "meaning of history" could almost be counted on the fingers of one hand. Since then, but particularly since the end of World War II, it has become difficult to keep abreast of even the bibliographies on the subject. The number of articles especially is abundant; and all points of view can be found expressed in contributions by men of such diverse persuasions as Roman Catholic, Protestant, existentialist, humanist, and Marxist.[1]

At first glance, then, it would seem that little can be added to the wealth of ideas which have gone before: one need only select the best of others' conclusions. Unfortunately it is not so simple as that. A closer look at these writings reveals that very little from a philosophical point of view has been published about the meaning of history. This is not surprising in the Protestant world, in the light of Karl Barth's prophetic writings about the cleavage between Christian faith and mundane events. But in the Catholic world, too, a genuine philosophy of history is so hard to find that M. C. Smit does not exaggerate when he says, "Since in Roman Catholic thought Christian reflection on history is primarily a matter of the *theology* of history and only exceptionally of its *philosophy*, the First Part will deal mainly with the *theology* of history" (author's translation).[2]

No doubt numerous non-Catholic authors will reject anything related to theology here; with Voltaire, the coiner of the term, they wish to present a pure "philosophy of history."[3] We can point to Condorcet, Turgot, Comte, Proudhon, Hegel, and Marx in the past, or to Litt, Jaspers, Heidegger, and Sartre in our own time. Careful scrutiny, however, will make clear the fact that the procedure adopted by these philosophers is not so exclusively philosophical as they assume or pretend. Expertly Karl Löwith has demonstrated how in their philosophies of history these thinkers rely upon an explicitly rejected but implicitly accepted theology. In his excellent *Meaning in History: The Theological Implications of the Philosophy of History*, he shows that the authors under discussion avail themselves of axiomatic theological implications as foundation stones for their philosophical theses.[4] A philosophical thesis, however, is only valid insofar as it is supported by philosophical argument; without that support it falls short of the requirements which the designation *philosophy* makes.

The thesis elaborately documented by Löwith is accepted as fact by other authors of widely divergent views. Romein, Litt, Vancourt—all maintain that the philosophy of history of Hegel and his followers is a secularization of the Christian view of history. We shall analyze this statement later, but our provisional conclusion must be that before we can speak of a philosophy of history with regard to these philosophers we must first investigate the claims of the term. Seeing that the philosophical value of their ideas is being challenged, we cannot very well take for granted that their ideas are truly philosophical ones.

There is another point. Löwith's own view, resulting from his investigation, is that only faith can grant an understanding of the sense of history; reason never can.[5] True, this author may be counted among the Protestant theologians, but even a High Churchman like C. S. Lewis calls the philosophy of history, not very flatteringly, a pseudoscience.[6] It is not unusual, either, for Catholic philosophers and theologians to deny that there exists such a thing as a philosophy of history. If they were right, there would be no point in continuing this discussion; but surely it behooves a philosopher to put the philosophical value of this opinion to the test. For the sake of brevity, I shall present here the negative views of a Catholic philosopher, the theories of a historian who is at the same time a theologian, the ideas of another theologian, and finally my own opinion and the argument upon which it is based. The attempt to refute the negative theses will conclude this section.

At the International Congress of Philosophy at Amsterdam, 1948, the Italian philosopher M. F. Sciacca contended that a

24

philosophy of history is the "vanity of vanities" because it will never be able to penetrate to the individual object of history. "What kind of dialectics can ever guide an individual's life and can solve the problems of man's destiny in this world—problems of evil, suffering and death—and of his ultimate goal?" (author's translation).[7]

Henri Marrou, the well-known French historian, acknowledges a critical philosophy of history which pertains to history as a discipline, but at the same time he denies the possibility of a philosophy of history which is concerned with history as a happening. In order to achieve such a philosophy we should be required to survey this happening in its entirety, according to him, an impossible demand of something which by its very nature implies an essential incompleteness. Only God knows history in its entirety, and only through God's revelation does the believer participate in his knowledge. This is why it is possible to have a theology of history but not a philosophy.[8]

Among the theologians, L. Malevez of Belgium agrees with the atheistic existentialists who proclaim the senselessness of human happenings, insofar, he specifies, as we should attempt a solution through human reason alone: "By definition and by its nature, metaphysics aims at wresting from the world its ultimate secret, its *absolute* sense; that is, the significance the world has for God himself" (author's translation).[9] But since such understanding is beyond human reason, he says that the only solution is to be found in faith: "But the significance which natural man fails to read in phenomena the believer affirms" (author's translation).[10]

These negative views will be considered and expanded on later; for the moment I shall just express my own point of view. Against the theologians—Catholics and Protestants alike—I should like to uphold the rights of a philosophy of history. Against such philosophers as deny the rights of theology I must point to the modest claims and the proper task of philosophy,

25

demonstrating the theological implications of their own systems. Against Catholic philosophers like Sciacca I proclaim the autonomy of Christian philosophy in this field too.

The philosophy of history does indeed exist; it has its own province which we are about to enter. But the ultimate and truly all-embracing truth about the meaning of history must be spoken by theology, by virtue of faith. Surely a philosopher may add here his opinion that theology cannot utter this word without availing itself, at least implicitly, of philosophy. I shall try to elucidate this in what follows.

The philosophical sense of history

In order to explain the paradoxical fact that history seems to have its origin in some particular "moment of history," Karl Jaspers in *The Origin and Goal of History* points to the following events as possible foundation stones: (1) the organization of river control and irrigation of the Nile, the Tigris-Euphrates, and the Hwang-ho, which enforced centralization, a civil service, and the formation of a state; (2) the discovery of writing, which was a necessary precondition for this organization; (3) the genesis of peoples with a common language, culture, and body of myths; (4) the organization of world empires, which prevented attacks on civilization by nomads; (5) the introduction of the horse either for drawing war chariots or for riding, which freed man from bondage to the soil.[11] The unsealing of history by these events leads inevitably to the question of what change in man occurred to cause his nebulous natural existence to pass into the realm of history. What was it in his nature that guided him toward history?

Jaspers mentions various factors here, but chief among them I consider man's self-awareness and his memory,[12] especially as we are speaking here of the essential nature of man. As primitive man became more aware of himself he grasped his link with the past and, taught by it, concerned himself with the future. His first technological achievements raised him above the momentary level and the pseudo-natural phase. Thus he came to life where history begins: in the triunity of past, present, and future.

In our time, finally, the history of man has merged into world history.[13] Whether we like it or not, whether we are in favor of isolation or cooperation, we are linked to the entire world. A conflict in faraway Vietnam is our concern, not only because we may be called into military service but also because of the resulting rise in prices in our country and others. At the time of the Suez affair, the dropping of English and French paratroopers caused a restriction of weekend driving in other corners of the world. In the fall of 1962, the discovery of missiles in Cuba brought a panic-stricken world to the brink of world war. Today our world is so technological and economic a whole that any form of isolation must be artificial and temporary. It is contrary to a unity which has already been realized—manifesting itself, unfortunately, most clearly in two *world* wars.

But these facts, marshaled here under Jaspers' inspiration, compel us to burrow deeper. How is it possible to arrive at "history" and "world history" as concepts unless they be already implied in man's nature? How, in our day, can the discovery be made that man not only *has* a history but *is* history,[14] unless this be no more than the revelation of man's essential being, of the phenomenon of man's nature? Consequently man, if he thus reveals himself in the present, cannot very well be (as regards his earthly being) anything but "a historic entity" (*ens historicum*). In an attempt to bring forward arguments for this viewpoint, I shall first deal with those based on scientific phenomenology. Hence the starting point will be experience.

Argument from scientific phenomenology

Man, we find, is a limited being. On probing into our limitations, we discover that we are limited not only generally (for example, because I am human I am not an angel) but more specifically (if I am a man, I am not a woman; if I am this man, I am not someone else). As an individual I am only an imperfect expression of man's perfection. The concept of man is reflected in the cracked mirror of myself. I owe my origin to others; I am surrounded by others; I have in me the power to work for others in the future for a posterity that is procreated materially, intellectually, and spiritually. In my individual self man is in no way fully grown. I am no more than a link in the ever-continuing, living chain of men.

The phenomenon of language, too, is instructive. I am a being who speaks, engages in dialogue, carries on conversations with others, uses language; but a living language presupposes "the other," the other to whom I can speak and who also speaks to me. The language which we speak we have received, as a rule, from our parents, other members of our families, our friends, our classmates and teachers. That language could not exist without those who preceded us. In the present, it should bear the stamp of our national genius, of which it is the expression; and it should enable us to pass it on, if possible in an enriched form, to those who come after us.

Were we to analyze numerous other factual experiences in the same way, we should always arrive at the same conclusion: I, as an individual, am a finite being; my being is a becoming. I am, in Heidegger's terms, someone cast, at his beginning, into the world; and my end is unavoidable. Meanwhile, in the interim, I am in the process of growing. In developing, while I tend toward the ultimate goal, the end, I cast a sidelong glance over my shoulder at the things that were; my eyes in the main on the future, I live in the present. Seen thus, "the present" is something more than a momentary instant; it is firmly linked on either side in the triad of past, present, and future. Being temporal, I live essentially in time. If, however, this growth in time is part of my external nature, if all these analyses show this to be revealed over and over again in my earthly appearance, then surely it is not rash to conclude that history is evidently part of my earthly being. I am a being who not only has a history but, at least in appearance, *is* history.

Argument from philosophical phenomenology

Nonetheless, if the present line of thought is to yield metaphysical certainty, one so unshakable that its denial would mean a negation of the intellect, it must also be valid on another plane. There, unlike in the preceding method, it will not derive its certainty from facts but, guided by those very facts, will attempt to arrive at its supratemporal truth. Not until it does so will our argumentation be fully metaphysical and phenomenological.

Let our starting point again be our own experience, the human spirit experiencing itself. Man in all his thoughts, acts, and modes of being is faced with his own limitations. I know myself, but at the same time this knowledge confronts me with my own inscrutability. My knowledge is never complete; each day I must discover myself again in order to arrive at a better knowledge of myself, a better self-possession by being more "myself." My doings, of course, are very closely related to my being. Each of my deeds bears witness to my limitations. No deed, however, exhausts the possibilities of my being. On the contrary, each one calls for new acts to make me more myself.

How do I acquire this deeper self-knowledge? How do I become more myself? Only by bringing myself into contact with, by surrendering myself to, that "other thing," the nonego, which has an existence of its own and opposes me. Let us for the moment denote all beings outside man "the world." Through my body, which belongs both to me and to that other thing, I am in contact with the world. I am dependent upon it; the only way I can exist is to accept and assimilate this dependence. Without a doubt I desire to be myself, to be free, to transcend my limitations, but I can only attain these desires by humbly surrendering

29

myself to the world. I must penetrate it with the light of my mind—I must make it susceptible to spiritual values—by my thinking and acting, working and loving. In order to arrive at myself I must go out to that other thing as a spirit into the world. I can only realize myself in the alienation of myself. My being is a becoming. My thinking and doing pass from thought to thought and from deed to deed, continually succeeding each other. Thus I become by succession; thus my being equals duration in succession. Now, "duration in succession" is a definition of *time*. Therefore, given my present earthly existence, I am always in a state of growth, of development, of evolution. But this evolution, this self-realization in time which makes of me a human being, is nothing but history. Man, therefore, as regards his earthly nature, is history, an *ens historicum*.

It might be objected that I have overreached myself. Since I have argued from the standpoint of *my* experience, cannot my only valid conclusion be that *I* am an *ens historicum*? The answer to this objection is that, while the experience which served as starting point was indeed my own, it was a metaphysical one; that is, an experience admittedly of my own individuality and temporality but one that at the same time transcended my individuality and temporality. It is in myself that I experience man's limitations as such because the human spirit and the world in themselves are our data. If my putting thoughts on paper is hindered both by a multitude of words and by the inadequacy of any of them to reproduce ideas exactly, it is not my individual experience that counts but the experience of being which is implied by that limitation.

In other words, my argument holds good for any other human being. We might even strengthen its reasoning by pointing out the fact that I become myself only by full abandonment to the world; that is, in abandonment of myself to "the other" and to his world I encounter both, starting from my world. Working involves interaction: cooperation or opposition. Loving—or hating—is first directed toward our fellowmen. Ultimately, it is the interhuman contact that matters. I become myself not only in relation to other *things* but especially in relation to "the other"; that is, my fellowman.

Accordingly, my conclusion is valid not only for myself but for man in the generic sense—as he takes his place in prehistory, history, and world history—for all mankind. Inherent in man is the need to realize, step by step in history, that he *is* history. It was as true for primitive man as it is for his modern counterpart, but we have become increasingly conscious of what has been embodied "from the beginning" in man's nature. For us moderns, man's appearance has contributed to a better understanding of his nature. Today the unity of mankind—a unity bestowed upon us by our belief in Christ and by that saving history which embraces the numerous histories of the nations and relates each to all others—is before our eyes; but its philosophical foundations rest upon the argument presented here. "Man realizes himself in time" corresponds with "Man realizes himself in history, *is* history" because the metaphysical argument holds good for man as man.

At the same time it will be clear, I hope, that this argument is fully valid for man alone. Only where man and the world— or more strictly speaking, mind and matter—are present together may we speak of self-possession in alienation, of duration in succession, of history in its proper sense. In God, pure spirit, the element of matter is absent. Consequently we cannot speak of history in relation to God. Nor can we with angels, on their plane, for analogous reasons. On the other hand, in the sphere of the subhuman there exists no spiritual element. For this reason there is no real opposition between plants or animals and their environment, the *Umwelt*—no alienation. There is only a "submersion" in matter. To be sure, in the sphere of the subhuman there is development, evolution; but even the animal, the highest form of life next to man, is not aware of this evolution.

Nor can it consciously contribute to this change. It is only the dynamic tension between mind and matter in the world which gives rise to the specific phenomenon denoted by the term *history*. It is possible, of course, to use the word in a derived sense in another context, by considering nature in its relation to man, but we must agree with Hegel's statement that organic nature has no history.[15]

The reader may find it easier to enter into this argument by bearing in mind that the conclusion that man realizes himself in time, is history, of necessity implies another truth: history has a purpose, a meaning.

The meaning of history

For the sake of clarity I shall begin this section by explaining the relationship between history and the meaning of history. This I shall follow with a brief outline of the various interpretations of the meaning of history, after which I shall resume my own argument.

What is the real meaning of such current catchphrases as *le sens de l'histoire, der Sinn der Geschichte, vom Ursprung und Ziel der Geschichte*, and "the meaning of history"? Malevez, speaking in a theological context, answers, "By the *sense* or *meaning* of history, they [the historians] would indicate, a little confusedly, its direction and even more its value as regards ultimate ends" (author's translation).[16]

Such vagueness is not accidental; it follows from the nature of history itself. In Löwith's words: "It is not by chance that we use the words 'meaning' and 'purpose' interchangeably, for it is mainly purpose which constitutes meaning for us . . . To venture a statement about the meaning of historical events is possible only when their *telos* becomes apparent."[17] Here meaning and purpose—the answers to Why? and Whither?—are obviously connected. Meaning is what gives history its purposeful content, what causes the shapeless mass of events to coalesce

32

into a whole which has at its center a single idea. This leads at once to a consideration of its purpose, which an ordered whole necessarily presupposes. If a multiplicity is to become a unity, it must have a specific direction.

In fact, it is impossible to speak about history without in so doing giving it at once a meaning and purpose. To begin with, the historian in his praxis cannot help introducing some degree of unity by categorizing time into such periods as the Middle Ages, the Renaissance, and the eighteenth century. This automatically implies an answer to the question about the meaning and purpose of each period. The answer may be provisional, or even incorrect, but it must be. This is true of every reflection upon history, even one not scientific. It would be true were a historian, declaring that mankind cannot be considered a whole, to deny that there is any meaning to history. His very reflection would be upon history as a whole—in that case, to judge it senseless. If its purpose were nothing, its aim nothing, meaning and purpose would be factually affirmed, even if they were repudiated in theory.

The logical necessity for history's being purposeful is contained in the metaphysical argument about man as an *ens historicum*. If man is to realize himself in time, if his essence is to be history, that history must have a purpose. Self-realization to be real (as it is here) assumes that it has a *finis*, a purpose. It must be directed toward something. Otherwise it is inactive, and self-realization, an activity, is not possible.

What, then, is the purpose in the case in point? Nothing less than man's self-realization, man's coming to be—not only in individual man, that is, but in man as such because our basic argument was concerned with man as man. Every individual is a limited realization of mankind, and it is in his multiplicity that man is forever attempting to transcend this limitation. Hence, if with Aquinas we consider mankind one man and if in respect of this analogy we call man's coming to be "a growing toward adulthood," we may define the meaning of history as "the process of man's growing toward adulthood."

Transcendence

This definition, however, does not remove our difficulties—far from it. On one hand, we are obliged to affirm an end or purpose which is essential to man's self-realization; we see this in man's coming to be, in his growth toward adulthood. On the other hand, we know only too well that this goal, mature manhood, can never be attained; it is simply beyond man's reach. Man on earth is always mind in matter, always capable of fuller realization in the "indefiniteness" of matter, always striving toward more nearly complete maturity, his new deeds penetrated by the light of the spirit. There is no end to this process of development because *complete man* is a contradiction of terms. This essential incompleteness concludes that history is necessary. To quote Jaspers: "Man's imperfection and his historicity are the same thing. . . . There is no perfect man."[18] Is it right, then, to adopt as a final purpose something obviously unattainable? Were it not more reasonable to accept history as meaningless, taking its course without finality?

An affirmative answer to these questions would make nonsense of our acquired certainties. The process of self-realization is real, and hence there must be a unifying purpose. This is Jaspers' view also, though he assumes an inascertainable *Grenzvorstellung* ("limit idea"), which exists as "truth" under its utterly false notional fixations.[19] Without arguing about the details of Jaspers' conception of symbol, which here come into play, I can concur in at least one respect: the ultimate, essential definition will not be found in man alone or in history seen exclusively as immanent. Like any limitation, self-realization necessarily points to transcendence. The immanence of man in history at the same time requires an affirmation of some reality transcending man, without which it could not be. We must still

34

qualify the purpose of history, therefore—namely, "the growth toward mature manhood"—by explicitly stating the transcendent implied in it. Here I depart from Jaspers. The very reason for assigning reality to this purpose is that to speak about a necessarily affirmed limit idea which has no content is to speak about something meaningless.

Thus, the purpose of history may be said to consist in man's development toward adulthood—one never to be attained by man alone, however, but to be found in *assimilatio Dei qua maxima*, "the greatest possible similitude to God." The process of man's ripening toward self-realization does not have its origins exclusively in man. The God who created him preceded him, and he is present at man's end. All history aims at man's achieving the greatest possible likeness to God. This end is metaphysical, no mere remote aim but a purpose ever present, ever more fully realized. Man is constantly becoming more himself; he comes more and more to resemble the image of God, his inmost core.

Therefore, we may say, using the traditional formula, that the purpose of history is "the glory of God," his increasing manifestation of himself. Although our immanent view remains paramount, it is man in the making who is a glorification of God, according to St. Irenaeus: *Gloria Dei vivens homo* ("Living man is God's glory").[20]

In my opinion, philosophy can do no more. When it has to decide at what point man reaches his greatest likeness to God, it is stymied. Such a final point must exist because the process is real, because man in the course of time shapes and reshapes himself; but to say precisely where that end lies is beyond the power of philosophy. Nor could it be otherwise because it is not for man to define the extent of his encounter with God. Only through God's revelation was St. Irenaeus granted the insight to continue his text with *Vita hominis visio Dei* ("Man's life is the vision of God").[21] According to the Christian faith, God's love for man is so great that he has sent his only Son, Jesus Christ, into the world to share the common lot of men and to deliver them from their miseries. In God incarnate man becomes God. No greater similitude of man to God can be found than in the person of Jesus Christ. In this historical fact, history has achieved its purpose.

Here we have entered the realm of theology. For a better understanding of the philosophical sense of history we shall have to venture into it again, but first we shall briefly consider the thoughts of the past about the meaning of history. They will enable us to see how much the philosophy of history owes to the answer that God gave us in his Son. Not until then shall we have a better understanding of the answer of philosophy, discerning the wide gap between this self-realization of man, his development toward maturity, and the concepts of the various philosophies of progress.

The Greek concept of history

It should be understood at the outset that *Greek* is used here in the broad sense. *Hellenistic* or *Greco-Roman* might be more exact terms. Contrasting the word with *Judeo-Christian*, however, I had in mind the biblical sense, as St. Paul's "to Jew first and then to Greek" (Romans 1:16). *Greek* here indicates the pagan way of living and thinking, which originated and centered in ancient Greece but which became more widespread in the last few centuries before Christ as the so-called Hellenistic civilization.

It is not easy to assess the Greek idea of history for "Hellenism has never succeeded in elaborating a philosophy of history, far less a theology of history" (author's translation).[22] Their idea of history was, as we shall see, one reason that we fail to find even a single articulated philosophy of history in any of the Greek philosophers' works. Statements made by them in other contexts, however, give us glimpses of their concepts of

36

history. This implicit philosophy or theology provides material for our argument. The Greek historiographers sometimes explicitly gave their outlook on the human events they narrated, an outlook which they evinced even in the way they told their stories. In the last analysis, however, we shall learn most in our search from the way in which the experience of history was manifest in Greek life. We can learn from their dramatists and poets, from their art, and above all from their religion, so intimately associated with their daily activities.

The Greeks exhibited a curious divergence of attitudes toward history. On one hand, we can see that the study of history had its origin, on the whole, with them. After Herodotus especially, many set out to describe their nation's past. The taste for history increased so greatly that the word ἱστορία, which originally meant no more than "inquiry" and could be applied to any branch of learning (as in περὶ τὰ ζῷα ἱστορία, "natural history"), came to mean without further qualification that part of knowledge concerned with the past. This development need not surprise us. The principal factor leading to the "origin" of history in mankind made itself felt in the Greek πόλις, the free city state, where writers began to reflect upon their relation to the past. Like future historians, the Greeks limited themselves in their practical study of history in order to deal with some particular whole which they could thus invest with a meaning.

On close study, however—and here we touch upon another contradiction in Greek attitudes toward history—it will become clear that the focus on a limited area never produced a comprehensive unity; nor was factual observation profoundly interpretative. In the historians' descriptions of a series of events, their perimeter was always narrowly bounded: the πόλις, the Expedition of the Ten Thousand, the creation of the nations of the Greeks or of the barbarians. Polybius—friend of Scipio Minor (circa 201-120 B.C.), the Greek hostage in Rome—even when he seemed aware of the interrelationship of the various national

37

histories, made no great improvement on this method. His planned history of the world (οἰκουμένη) was merely the story of the origins and development of the Roman Empire. Everything in his narrative was directed toward the realization of the Empire as toward a single purpose (τέλος). Even his wider vision did not range beyond the contemporary issues of his time. His outlook, like that of his predecessors, was curiously occupied with the past only.

No doubt we can learn about the past to the advantage of the present, as can be seen in Thucydides' writings, but Greek history for the main part lacked the signposts pointing toward the future. The only dimensions with which Greece's historians were familiar were the past and the present; the future, without which dimension the other two could not have true unity, did not exist for them. Even their literature utilized worn plots. The main concern of tragedy was not the denouement but rather the "how" of the play. The Greeks lived in "the grip of the past," Van Groningen aptly puts it.[23] The reasons for this preoccupation with the past were expressly given by the historiographers of the period. They said that all human events occurred in a cycle, in the eternal return of all things. "I would tell you," Herodotus admonished, "human life is like a revolving wheel and never allows the same man to continue long in prosperity."[24] Thucydides' celebrated κτῆμα ἐς αἰεί ("a lasting possession") rested on the same idea of all events' recurrence.

> It will be enough for me, however, if these words of mine are judged useful by those who want to understand clearly the events which happened in the past and which (human nature being what it is) will, at some time or other and in much the same way, be repeated in the future. My work is not a piece of writing designed to meet the taste of an immediate public but was done to last forever.[25]

In Polybius this fundamental attitude was in no way modified: "This is the cycle of public institutions, the organization

38

of Nature, that the various shapes of states will change and pass over into others and revert again to their origin."[26] Even in that romanized Hellene the idea of a unique purposeful happening in human existence as a whole was absent. This stems from the Greek concept of time, which—notwithstanding the fact that the Greeks clung to the past or rather because they did so—was antihistorical. What was characteristic of archaic man in general was manifestly true of them, even at the supreme phase of their civilization.

What, then, were their ideas about time? Strictly speaking, this is the wrong kind of question here, incompatible as it is with the state of mind which we are to examine. The early Greeks in particular were unaware of thought as a function to be distinguished from feeling and acting. As primitives, they lived in an undifferentiated whole of feeling, thinking, acting, and worshiping. They were in original harmony with nature and saw their life take its course according to that rhythm. Archaic man witnessed the constant recurrence of seasons, the rising and setting of the sun. In the lunar cycle, above all, he saw exemplified the death and return to life of all beings. Such was his view of nature, of the true life, of man himself: all things are born, live, die, and come to life again. To Homer—the "child-poet," as Ernest Hello once called him—the idea was a living reality:

> As the growth of leaves, so are the generations of man;
> If the wind shakes down the leaves on the earth, a new foliage
> Sprouts from the budding wood when spring returns.
> So one generation of mortals waxes, another one fades. [Author's
> translation.][27]

This was the way in which primitive man passed through time, not linearly, not with a definite purpose, but in an endless cycle having neither beginning nor end, recurring forever.

Does this mean that to Homer all human acts were devoid of meaning? Not absolutely. An event had "significance" as a mundane reiteration of a divine occurrence. The individual and

39

the world of human events, however, had no worth in themselves, but they acquired value as reflections of things divine. Reality, according to the belief of primitive peoples, was to be found in some primordial occurrence. The earth, like a womb, contained all future events; nothing new could be born of it. Everything was a repetition of what had happened before. Such repetition might tend to be either static in its symbolism (even buildings and their sites pointed to the supra-terrestrial center) or dynamic (certain rituals consciously recalled the Deity's primal act).[28] Such representation was effected by myth.

Of the various dictionary definitions of *myth*, that of "fictitious story" may be uppermost in our minds. This is because our knowledge of the term derives mainly from "mythology," those tales, dissociated from their origin, which have come down to us in a body. Archaic man, however, had no such collection. He knew the myths in their origins because he was a part of them. To him a myth was a truth.[29] He did not reflect upon a myth's nature; he lived it. Were we to identify ourselves with him, we should discover, with anthropologists and students of comparative religion, that a myth is no mere prehistorical story, no metaphorical explanation of the origin of the world and of man, not just a word (etymologically, it is derived from μῦδος, "word"). It is an act, a gesture, through which primal events are again presented to us. Against all tendencies toward intellectualism, M. Leenhardt's interpretation is that "A myth is felt and lived before being circumscribed and formulated. It is the word, the shape, the gesture, which circumscribes the event in the heart of man, emotive as a child, before becoming a fixed story" (author's translation).[30]

Through myth archaic man transcended historical time and reiterated the event thus embodied.

A sacrifice, for example, does not only reproduce exactly the initial sacrifice revealed by some god *ab origine*, in the beginning of time, but, moreover, it takes place at that same mythical pri-

mordial moment. In other words, every sacrifice repeats the initial
sacrifice and coincides with it . . . profane time and duration
being suspended by the paradox of rite.[31]

Profane time, as we experience it, was suspended by this excursion into mythical time. It was only through this unifying reiteration that man, returning to his origins, became himself. Only on
a few occasions in his life did man return to his beginnings, but
it was to these times that he and the world around him owed
their existence. The festivities, commemorations, and sacrifices
of worship returned in a certain order of succession. By celebrating these festivities, man restored the reality which they
symbolized, a reality in danger of being lost. The celebrations
introduced nothing really new, but the participants experienced
a mundane repetition of pre-temporal, divine events. Every New
Year's Day was a recurrence of the genesis of the world which
was in danger of dying. It was reborn, thanks to this feast and
the other red-letter days of the year. The festive calendar is by
its nature limited, repeating itself after having once revolved.
Thus, through the mythical way, we too arrive at the circular
concept of time. Man is enclosed and preserved within the unity
of nature's cycle.[32]

Next, Greek man attained to greater self-awareness, pro-
ceeding, Nestle says, *Vom Mythos zum Logos* (From Myth to
Reason); but this is not to imply the complete defeat of myth,
as that author, arguing from his own rationalistic system, would
have it.[33] No doubt myth had now lost its monopoly and was
viewed more and more merely as literature, apart from its action. It became a subject for the imagination of poets and,
later, an object of mockery for sophists. But the genuine philosophers—Socrates, Plato, Aristotle—would not reject the myths
in their entirety, those "truths . . . of inspiring vision and . . .
unerring anticipation" (author's translation).[34] Just as we cannot understand their predecessors without regarding them as
men making their first attempts at disengagement from mythical

41

thinking—men still living in that unbroken unity of slowly differentiating myth—in order never to forget that these φυσικοί ("physicists") were at the same time θεολόγοι ("theologians"), so should we regard the triad of Socrates, Plato, and Aristotle in relation to the pre-Socratics and their underlying concepts. Plato was very clear on this point. He knew the critique of the sophists and partly agreed with it, but he rejected their rationalistic pseudo-autonomy. Aware of his own inadequacies, he did on occasion have recourse to the root of his own thought, to myth. This was not, however, to accept uncritically the creations of popular or poetic imagination.

> Now, it would not be fitting for a man of sense to maintain that all is just as I have described it, but that this or something like it is true concerning our souls and our abodes, since the soul is shown to be immortal, I think he may properly and worthily venture to believe; for the venture is worth while.[35]

Thus Plato, at the height of the symposium, had Socrates (that is, philosophy) expound the idea of philosophy by restating what he had heard from the priestess Diotima (that is, religion). Myth, in Plato's philosophy, retained its essential place at the root of things.

This may be less true of Aristotle. We can unfortunately do no more than touch on this matter here and must refer the interested to Werner Jaeger, an expert on the subject of Aristotle, for the Stagirite's attitude toward myth. Jaeger's verdict is that Aristotle always philosophized along the lines of the Anselmian *credo ut intelligam* ("I believe in order to understand").[36] This bold dictum is only cited here to throw some doubt on the possible conception of a purely autonomously thinking Aristotle. Such doubts can only be heightened when we consider that Aristotle was a pupil of Plato for twenty years, that in his own dialogues he used myths as Plato did, that he was slow to diverge from his master and, to all intents and purposes, never came to oppose him completely. He is the first

Greek, according to Jaeger, to see the world through Plato's eyes, and consequently we should not be surprised to read in his *Metaphysics*, "For that reason the lover of myth is to a certain extent a philosopher" (author's translation).[37] Aristotle too saw an element of philosophical truth in myth.

Having seen, then, how even at the high tide of Greek thought people remained loyal to myth, we shall have a better understanding of how they, their predecessors, and those who followed them kept alive the myth of eternal return as an under-lying pattern of thought. Their idea of time was cyclical. It will become clear how, implicitly or explicitly, their idea of history continued to be essentially the same as the mythical awareness of their primitive ancestors. When they stated these views, they may have done so in various forms. The primordial events were straightforwardly indicated as "prehistoric," but the cyclical idea can be traced back more often in the tendency to refer, wherever possible, everything to antiquity, considering whatever was old the best: τιμιώτατον γὰρ τὸ πρεσβύτατον ("for the oldest is the most honorable"). Aristotle's expression, which Van Groningen took as motto for an essay, is but the expression of a generally held idea, as is shown in numerous other quotations. The argument for this position is likewise given in Aristotle's τὸ ἀρχαῖον ἐγγύς τι φαίνεται τοῦ φύσει ("Antiquity is nearer to nature").[38] Herein was implied the idea that the world was de-generating, that a decline was unavoidable. Hesiod was the first Greek to voice this contention, when he analyzed his five (or four) great periods consecutively. Ovid too described these ages in declining sequence: gold, silver, bronze, heroic, and iron. Human history, the entire world of becoming, thus is of inferior value. When, therefore, the Greeks came to reflect on this happening, they saw reality only in another world, in com-plete rest and immutability. To them, the world of the stars mov-ing in their fixed tracks showed the most nearly perfect imitation of this permanence. Time, according to the *Timaeus*, was

43

"a kind of mobile image of eternity" (author's translation).[39] A consequence of this perfection was, however, that even a straight line in this world of types, was imperfect. The fates of men and stars were caught in the same iron grip. Whatever was new or surprising was declared nonexistent: "All things are always the same, and neither now nor afterwards will there be anything more than there was before" (author's translation), Lucretius said.[40] The varying elaborations of this fundamental concept show how many held that the diverse cycles in which different worlds spin contained the selfsame events. For that reason, Aristotle (or the author of the *Problemata*) stated that we cannot, strictly speaking, call times "former" or "later." While we can legitimately consider ourselves existing after the Trojan War, for example, in another sense our activities take place before that time. This does not foolishly assert that, numerically speaking, the same men are born again and again. It is safer to say that they return in species (τῷ εἴδει).[41]

Clear philosophical amplifications of the cyclical interpretation of history are, of course, supplied by the history of philosophy. We need only, for example, think of Pythagoras, of Heraclitus ("the road downwards, the road upwards"), of the four realms of Empedocles which had their origin in the continuous struggle between love and hate, of the Stoa doctrine of ever-recurring worldwide conflagration, and of the return of things to their origin as taught by the neo-Platonists. But even where a philosophical explanation does not suggest itself, the problem of the interpretation of history should be seen against the mythical background of the cycle.

This is not to say that we find, at no time or place, any Greek idea of progress. In fact, Siegfried Lauffer, at the Brussels International Congress of Philosophy, 1953, pointed out some instances.[42] It is difficult to accept a view, however, which speaks of a "totally different concept," even while acknowledging with Lauffer that the ancients' "progress" was no more than partial and that the Greeks only tried to bring their optimistic ideas into accord with the cyclical theory, which they never abandoned. It is as if the *anima naturaliter christiana* was making itself felt in the efforts of many who strove to alter the old ideas, even those about progress. Only when the Redeemer appeared from the transcendent, however, could they be released from the magic spell of the cycle. This struggle was exemplified in Plato's interpretation of history, in which he saw an interruption of the cycle at one point, where individual immortality was concerned, but this interruption was only partial and incidental. Personal immortality, subsequent on reincarnation, was reserved for the souls of philosophers who would retain the happiness that they had once enjoyed.[43] Apparently, even Plato found the idea of something new unacceptable.

Summing up its philosophical implications, we find that the mythical cycle (a) hindered belief in a personal God and individual free will in assuming that all was governed by the cycle, fate ruling man and gods alike, (b) was incompatible with the idea of creation in that it ruled out anything new, (c) precluded personal immortality (that is, the attainment of a final state previously unknown to the individual), (d) deprived mundane life and human events of their immanent sense, thus leading, on deeper reflection, to a radical religious or philosophical dualism, (e) undervalued things singular and individual and the knowledge of such as compared to things universal.

It is remarkable that the cyclical concept in various forms continued to be the one dominant in the world, except for the perspective on history afforded by Judaism and Christianity. "The interest in the irreversability and the 'newness' of history is a recent discovery in the life of mankind."[44]

The Judeo-Christian concept of history

Mircea Eliade may rightly speak of a "young" discovery in the life of mankind, although the Jewish concept of history is

45

rather old. It did not become familiar and was not perfected until the rise of Christianity, which brought to the face of the earth an entirely new concept of time and history.

The cyclical concept was replaced by a linear one. This Christian interpretation was, however, the fulfillment of the expectation that was alive in Israel. That is why the whole of Christianity is unintelligible apart from some knowledge of the nation which was to give the world the Messias. In order to understand Christianity we must first consider Judaism and its unique idea of time, though not at great length for surely we are on familiar ground here. I should like to point out in advance, however, that my interpretation of Israel's history is not accepted by present-day Jewish theologians, many of whom even reject the idea of a personal Messias.

The Jewish nation lived by virtue of, and for the sake of, its history. The Dutch exegete and present cardinal, Bernard Alfrink, has drawn attention to the fact that amidst its oriental neighbors Israel was the only nation familiar with history; that is, history in the sense of historiography (quite distinct from a mere chronicle of contemporary events) as well as history seen as the interpretation of mundane events. The typical difference between it and the Greek view, wherever each reflected on the past, is that to Israel the past was not important merely as the life story of their ancestors; it had value for the present and even more for the future. Israel was aware that it was making its own history or, rather, that Yahweh was making the history of this nation, at least the history of the "remnant" that had remained faithful to him. Yahweh's revelation, too, had brought the nation to the conclusion (inexplicable from a purely human standpoint) that the history of Israel concerned not only its own people but all, seeing that Yahweh, whom all nations were to serve, had chosen Israel for his people above all other nations. Israel was familiar with world history because its history was important to the world.

46

Jewish history represents an essential and complete break with the cyclical concept held by the Greeks. It knew of a beginning: the creation of a heaven and earth by a personal God who had as his special concern the welfare of the world and of every single human being in it. With the Fall a promise was given which had an eschatological vista: complete victory over evil. Man's repeated unfaithfulness was followed by the Flood, from which Noah and his family were saved in order to reveal God's purpose. With the Covenant, the blessing of Shem, and the election of the Jewish people (through Abraham's call from Ur to Canaan), was made manifest the will of God that Israel should be a great nation through which all generations of the earth should be blessed. The exodus from Egypt into the promised land, a lapse into unfaithfulness and the renewal of the covenant following repentance, ever-stronger conviction that the new heaven and earth in the days of the Messias were near, expectation of the day of Yahweh and the end of time—these successively carried history toward fulfillment. The end would be no mere reinstatement of the beginning, although the prophets understandably chose to couch references to man's ultimate state of happiness in terms which would be familiar to their audience. It was to be an end toward which all preceding events had pointed and toward which Yahweh himself had lovingly and unerringly been leading his people because he wanted to redeem them.

The difference between the Jewish and the Greek concepts is clearly shown in how each interpreted the idea of the four realms. The Greeks saw the ages as progressively degenerating; and while an apparent parallel to this view can be seen in Daniel 2:31 ff. and 7:13, there is a difference in the Jewish view. After the realm of iron and clay, "the God of heaven will set up a kingdom that shall never be destroyed or delivered up to another people." The kingdom of the Son of Man was to "stand forever."

We also see that the line as a concept was no simple, undeviating one. In fact, the history of Israel is the story of relapsing and rising again. Daniel spoke of a decline. Nevertheless, we can and must speak of a linear concept of history, as opposed to the cyclical one of the Greeks, because Yahweh's intervention, despite his people's human failings, kept the path straight. The definite goal, the eschatological realm, was always beckoning. Nor should we consider the contrast between the Jewish and the Greek concepts so definite as to exclude every mythical element from Jewish thought. Over and over again we read in the Scriptures that in Israel the multitude was bent on escaping into myth, turning from history and vocation in history, and had to be reminded of duty by the few. In fact, there is even an explicit description of the eternal cycle in the first chapter of Ecclesiastes: "Nothing is new under the sun." But just as the infidelities of Israel must be viewed within the framework of Yahweh's basically straight line, so must we consider the Preacher's words about the passing away of generations of men on a permanent earth within the context of his pessimistic admonitions concerning the vanity of human life and human deeds, and within the frame of reference of the entire Old Testament.

The last vagueness to be found in Israel's concept of history was to disappear, however, with the coming of Christ, the Son of Man. When the time was ripe, the Word of God became man, through the consent of Mary, the representative of her people (Israel and, vicariously, all mankind) and by the overshadowing of the Holy Ghost.

> God, who at sundry times and in divers manners spoke in times past to the fathers by the prophets, last of all in these days has spoken to us by his Son, whom he appointed heir of all things, by whom also he made the world (Hebrews 1:1-2).

With his coming, life, preaching, cross, and resurrection, redemption was achieved—ἅπαξ, "once for all" (Romans 6:10; Hebrews 7:27, 10:10; 1 Peter 3:18). Here the Greek concept was completely abandoned. It was not the past which contained perfection but the present. The Old Testament was an imperfect prefigurement of what was yet to come. The Greeks knew the perfect primal image, which was only imperfectly imitated and repeated. The image of the invisible God, in the Judeo-Christian tradition, was a fulfillment of what had been promised. Beyond Christ, the Son of God, immanent in the universal history of mankind, we cannot go. In him we have received all things. Human history has attained fulfillment in the God-man, Jesus Christ, the alpha and the omega, the beginning and the end.

Does this mean that since Christ's leaving the earth history has become meaningless? Are we to fall back on the repetition of the Greeks? By no means. On the contrary, the historical fact of the Incarnation of God has radically changed the concept of time, bestowing on each moment an eternal value. Since the Ascension, the Church, his Bride, has preserved the three dimensions of history: Jesus Christ is the same yesterday, today, and in eternity. The Church will be living at the end of time, as she does in the present. Glancing toward the past wherein his coming was prepared for, she at the same time faces the future. According to Scripture, the passion of Christ did not complete his body, the Church. Therefore is creation still in travail; we are responsible for the completion of the body. But while Christendom longs earnestly for completion, it knows that this end cannot be accomplished without Christ's return, and for this event do we pray. Christ's final appearance as judge, however, will be quite different from his coming as redeemer to Bethlehem. The new event, the ultimate one in history, will be the completion which all the foreshadowings have prophesied.

The intermediary period, then, is far from meaningless but is highly purposeful because its progress and final event are determined by the Lamb, who has been slain and is therefore considered worthy to open the book. For the Lord of history to open the book means for him to shape history. This he accomplishes by staying with his Church, continuing to work in his members. They may have confidence in their ability to achieve this work because he has already conquered the world. It is left to them only to consolidate this victory in time. The final vision of the Apocalypse, where the biblical view of history finds its most detailed and profound interpretation, is of the Holy City, the New Jerusalem, where the Bride of the Lamb is to be adorned with God's glory. All former things will have passed away; everything will have been made new. God's people will know the ineffable bliss of being with their God. Not until then will the Bride be able to repeat the words of her Bridegroom, "It is finished," or to speak more theocentrically with St. Paul: "Then comes the end, when he delivers the kingdom to God the Father, when he does away with all sovereignty, authority and power. . . . that God may be all in all" (1 Corinthians 15:24-28). This should not be interpreted as a return to the cyclical idea. No, the straight historical line—provided it is understood in its metaphorical sense, with the implication that even the deviations caused by sin do not essentially impair its general course because Christ has conquered sin—is maintained in the period between the first and the second coming, our present era.[45] Mankind does not return to a God in whom it preexisted but finds its completion through Christ in its Creator, to whom it owes the newness and uniqueness of its existence. In order to be definitively united with him, this earth of man, sin, and time must be transformed into a new heaven and earth in eternity. In Christ and in his Mother, this has already taken place. Through their personal cooperation the Redemption is worked out in the members of Christ's body, the Church.

Historical outline of the philosophy of history

These Christian truths have redeemed human thought from its cyclical course, confronted it with the phenomenon of history in its fullest sense, and thus directed it first to a theology of history, next to a philosophy, and even to a mode of thought that explicitly rejects this redeeming faith but implicitly lives by it. It would be interesting to investigate the power of thought engendered in mankind by these truths. How many shades of meaning have the theology and philosophy of history known since their Christian origins? How many ramifications are still being developed in Christianity's ever-changing newness, particularly in our time? Here, however, I shall follow my original plan of presenting a brief outline of history for a better understanding of my personal view of the philosophy of history. In recalling that the idea of a cyclical course of history was not wholly abandoned in Christianity, we need only think of Origen, Siger of Brabant, and Vico. To the background of the Christian linear view some cyclical or spiral aspects would not be inadmissible, since the straight line is not to be interpreted in the sense of a naïve sort of progress, but as a basic attitude the cyclical concept is contrary to the Christian faith.

Augustine, after Irenaeus, has been the great champion of the straight line: "Augustine's *City of God* (412-426) is the pattern of every conceivable view of history that can rightly be called 'Christian.' "[46] The bishop of Hippo was the first great theologian of history. His interpretation of its meaning was to dominate Western thought for centuries. It even penetrated the secularized philosophy of history. In twelve chapters of the *City of God* (10-21 of Book XII), he circumstantially refuted the Greek concept and offered instead his own theology of history: "Let us follow the straight way, which for us is Christ. May he lead and redeem us from the circular course of the heathens" (author's translation).[47]

There is nothing surprising in the fact that Augustine, an ardent lover of Christ, considered Christ the pivot of world history. He worked out his idea logically. Five periods preceded Christ's coming: from Adam to the Flood, from Noah to Abraham, from Abraham to David, from David to the Babylonian captivity, and from the captivity to Christ. In Christ mankind became one; hence Augustine considered these periods analogous to the growth of individual man, passing through stages of *infantia, pueritia, adolescentia, iuventus,* and *virilitas* before attaining the final stage of life. This final era, of indefinite duration, will close with the second coming of Christ. It is called *senectus,* "old age," seeing that it extends to the end of time. It is also, to us a more theological term coined by the father of Hippo, the "time of grace." In this period the battle between the "City of This World" and the "City of God" (that terrestrial reflection of the communities of darkness and of light in the angelic realm) is in full swing. The battle first manifested itself in the quarrel between Cain and Abel, but the ultimate victory of the heavenly city is ensured; in truth, it has already been gained by Christ. Christ, mature man, has preserved the unity of history. Augustine made no place for the interruption of a seventh period of peace and rest, about which the millenarians dream. In Christ, mankind has arrived at the end of time. We are old, and we are weary with waiting for the eternal rest of the sabbath:

> But this seventh period will be *our* sabbath. It will not end at night but at our Lord's day, as an eternal eighth day sanctified by Christ's resurrection, symbol of an eternal rest for soul and body. Then we shall test and see, see and love, love and praise. That will be our endless end. [Author's translation.][48]

When mankind had grown older by some centuries, its concept of age was to change from Augustine's view. People became increasingly attentive to what was taking place on earth, at the same time acquiring "an existential sense of the past" (author's translation), as Ariès has it.[49] Nevertheless, Augustine's theology of history was fundamentally upheld by the Schoolmen. Rejection of its essential traits—the battle between the two "cities," the victory gained in Christ, life at the end of time—would signify the end of Christianity itself. This is what excited the mild-natured Aquinas to use such invectives as "vanity" and "most stupid" in refuting the doctrine of Joachim of Fiore (1131-1202).[50] This Cistercian monk expected, after the realm of the Father in the Old Testament and the realm of the Son in the New Testament, a third and final period, the realm of the Spirit. Aquinas argued that in this life a closer to perfect state than that of the new law could not possibly exist because through Christ we were immediately introduced to eternal life. After his Resurrection and Ascension, the Holy Ghost was granted us at once. "This likewise rules out the fallacies of anyone, whoever it be, who says that there will be another period, of the Holy Ghost" (author's translation). What is more, another law, the gospel of the Holy Ghost, is not possible.

> As for the fourth objection, the reply is as follows. Because Christ at the very beginning of his preaching the gospel has said, "The kingdom of heaven has approached," it is the height of stupidity to assert that the gospel of Christ is not the gospel of the kingdom. [Author's translation.][51]

In spite of the secularistic humanist historiographers and the excellent, fundamentally new philosophy of history worked out by Giovanni Battista Vico, his somewhat older contemporary Bossuet continued to pattern himself after Augustine, even in such relatively unessential features of the philosophy of history as periodization. True, the contemporary of Louis XIV paid more attention to mundane events than had medieval historiographers, but in fact his *Discours sur l'histoire universelle* (A Treatise on Universal History) of 1681 constituted "the last theology of history on the pattern of Augustine."[52] Voltaire, in his *Essai sur les moeurs et l'esprit des nations* (Essay on the Manners and Spirit of Nations), wrote its sequel in 1765, beginning where Bossuet had left off, with Charlemagne. He intended nonetheless to refute Bossuet's theology by this first "philosophy of history." "We are going to speak of Jews as if we were speaking of Scythians or Greeks," he wrote.[53]

53

It is not my intention to record here all the philosophical pronouncements on the meaning of history made by Voltaire and others in the days of the Enlightenment. Nor will I demonstrate how all these philosophies lived thanks to the grace of dogmas explicitly rejected by them; Löwith has already done this. I merely wish to present a few examples from history to illustrate my thesis, going into detail only in the case of Hegel, the most brilliant of these thinkers, and his view of history. The naïve optimistic belief in the continuous progress of a humanity which found itself freed from the fetters of dogma has been sadly refuted by the facts. A more rational version of the idea of purely human progress is still alive in the modern adherents of the philosophies of Hegel and Marx. In their philosophy of history we shall discover the apex of rationalism. Hegel was fascinated by contemporary political events; it is only when we consider this fact that we can understand his philosophy of history. Consider this in the strongly religious light in which he regarded mundane events, and you will arrive at a better comprehension of why, on one hand, history came to be the seminal factor in his philosophy and, on the other, history in Hegel was the external realization of the absolute spirit. His *Philosophie der Geschichte* (The Philosophy of History) was substantially influenced by Herder and Vico, the latter of whom emerged from obscurity thus.

Human thought, according to Hegel's profound analysis, is essentially a dialectical process of thesis-antithesis-synthesis. We know truth but only in the course of development. Hence it follows that objective reality, too, is subject to this dialectical development. "The true is the whole."[54] It is essential "to interpret the true not as substance but just as much as subject and to express it this way" (author's translation).[55] To Hegel the spirit was essentially historical; only in the dialectical process was it realized. This held for the human spirit, for the spirit as such, for the externalization of the human spirit as it is found in history. The aim of history was the being-in-and-for-itself of the spirit in complete freedom. The way this was attained was the compulsory course of the dialectical process by means of which the spirit developed toward ever-increasing liberty. The origin of all history, the thing which made history possible from the moment when man came into being, Hegel said in his *Phänomenologie des Geistes* (Phenomenology of Spirit), was strife. Divested of all technical details, his widely known dialectic comes down to this: Two prehistoric creatures —"premen," if you like, creatures still one with organic nature and incapable of rising above it—met and engaged in struggle. If in this fight one killed the other, the victor remained contained in nature, the same preman he was. There is another possibility. It may be that the weaker of the two in a flash of mortal anguish had borne upon him the necessity of surrender and, in acknowledging the other stronger, made the victor aware of his power. Thus the stronger arrived at self-consciousness. He was capable of annihilating or sparing his victim and so was superior to him. Thus he *was.* In saving his victim he became himself, the master; he existed for himself. The other, in his submission, accepted living for his master; he was the slave who existed for the other.[56]

Thus begun, the history of mankind, according to Hegel, was of all things a manifestation of the one *Weltgeist* ("world spirit"), which worked itself up to ever-greater freedom via numerous *Volksgeister* ("spirits of the people"). Of course, Hegel was giving a personal and contemporary view of history. In the oriental world, he believed, people were ignorant of the fact that man as such was free. They knew that *one* was free, but this was the freedom of the despot, not truly a free person. The consciousness of freedom arose with the Greeks, but this consciousness did not extend beyond the idea of freedom for *some* rather than for man as such. Hence slavery continued to exist for them, and individual freedom was no more than relative.

The awareness of true freedom was finally recognized by the Germanic peoples, influenced as they were by Christianity. They came to learn that man as man is free, that freedom of spirit is essential to his being. This idea, too, took time to be realized in practice, but at least it existed in principle.[57]

The most important form in which Hegel's philosophy of history survives today is Marxism. To be sure, the claims that Marx was a great philosopher can be waved airily away. It is possible to relegate his name, in a handbook on modern philosophy, to an occasional reference or to omit it altogether. Such a theoretical evaluation, however, is of little significance in the face of the undeniable fact that Marx's interpretation of the meaning of history is regarded by millions as a gospel of redemption from the senselessness and misery of their lives.

Marx took over Hegel's dialectics, but he reversed the content of the latter's philosophy, as it were. It is not mind which is the power behind history but matter, even if it be that this matter is seen in its unity with man. In Marxism the process of man's realization of himself and of the origins of history are located in the second phase of Hegel's master-and-slave dialectics. In the shaping of matter the slave becomes man, in the same way as matter is realized by this process. Hence Marx's view of the three great periods of history was utterly different from Hegel's, though the two appear to have the same ultimate purpose: the attainment of complete human freedom. For Marx the first period was the precapitalist era, in which everybody worked to obtain the fruit of his labors as private property. Next, as antithesis, came the capitalist era, in which the many workers were robbed of their gains by a small minority, who were in possession of the capital and were continuously adding to it. The synthesis is the communist era, in which everybody works, and everybody possesses goods, collectively.

The road toward this final, ideal phase is the irrevocably dialectical procedure in which the way of production of material goods is decisive for the mode of existence of human society. By evolution and revolution of the productive process, this society will be transformed under the dictatorship of the proletariat into a classless society, "in which the free development of each is a condition for the free development of all."[58]

Even from this thumbnail sketch, which of course falls short of Hegel's and Marx's brilliant conceptions, it may be inferred, I hope, how important their philosophies of history have been. In the twentieth century, their ideas have penetrated much more deeply than they did in their own time. Primarily because of them we now understand that man is a historical being. The aspect of truth in their philosophies has been definitely incorporated as an essential element of the *philosophia perennis* ("eternal philosophy"). Nevertheless, Hegel's and Marx's arguments did not run entirely parallel with those of their contemporary philosophers. Much less do their views resemble ours. In their philosophies of history rationalism reached its culmination point. By this I mean that their views are the most positive, if not the best, representatives of the attempt made in their time to interpret history by means of natural reason alone. Now let us take a closer look at their points of view, which will enable us to realize better why their viewpoints, in spite of the precious aspects of truth in them, fall short in the apprehension of reality—and why Marx's philosophy can offer no more than a spurious salvation.

Hegel, as Marx, differs from most philosophers of the Enlightenment because he does not consider history a process of everlasting progress but sees it as purposive. Thus for Hegel this means the complete presence, in full liberty, of the spirit; for Marx it is the unrestricted development of every individual in a classless society. Both understand very well that if the process of evolution in history is to be a real one, it must have a purpose. On this issue they agree with the old Christian concept as put forward by St. Augustine. But the great difference is that

57

this purpose is secularized by Hegel and Marx and that they see it as purely human, of this world. Together with Voltaire and his adherents they look for human perfection solely in man. However, not a single reasonable argument can be brought forward in support of the thesis that the triad will stop at Prussia (according to Hegel the perfect state), at Lutheranism (the perfect religion), at Hegel's philosophy as the perfect philosophy, or at Marx's imaginary condition of happiness. This, too, is a synthesis which, on account of its human origin, bears the seeds of another antithesis in itself. The Absolute will never be reached in the present world, which will always be "unfinished and unfinishable."[59]

But this is no more than to say that the terminal point of Hegel's process, in spite of all his talk about absolutivity, is only relative—which causes the entire process to become relative and to lose its sense and, consequently, its reality. Hegel is, of course, an outstanding philosopher of history, but in fact his sense of history destroys history itself. His answer is that the process will continue even after his death, that things have reached their end only in principle. A philosopher has to furnish proof of his answers, and this is where Hegel fails. The dogma of the fulfillment of all in Christ is secularized into the unproven postulate of fulfillment in Hegel. Even then there remains the philosophical short circuit: a purely human purpose can never give a transcendent sense to history.

We can argue in a similar way against Marx. The first question to ask of Marx, as of Hegel, is Why is the dialectical process stopping at this final point, and why is not the Communist society, in its turn, passing into its contrary via a revolution? We may assume that the answer will be that this very end is the beginning of the truly human condition and of real history. In my opinion, however, the crux of the matter is the demonstration that, on the one hand, the dialectical process, bringing about man's self-realization, has come to an end and that, on the other hand, man continues to be formed. How can we prove rationally that we really have to do with the beginning of a new era, one in which the old rules of dialectics for man and matter are no longer valid and one in which new man leads a new life? No doubt we might explain this as a secularization of Marx's Jewish faith in a messianic era, but certainly this would not be in agreement with Marx's rational philosophy.

Accordingly, it is easy to understand that post-Marx Marxists, especially now that Communist sovereignty in Soviet Russia has come to stay, are wondering how the continuation of history is to be justified. Stalin, in particular, occupied himself with this problem. His attempted solution was that Communist society be kept astir. Even a revolutionary process ought to be directed from above. In consequence the superstructure, the ideology, would become more and more important.[60] A highly interesting view, no doubt, but the question remains of how far such a reflection on history still concurs with Marx's view, whether it is still consistently keeping to his line. In a certain sense it is, insofar as new rules of being are in force, now that the purpose of history has been attained in the Communist ideal State. This makes particularly clear how strongly Marxism draws on the inspiration of the messianic final time. On the other hand, Marx's view of the dialectical process in history has lost all its validity here; it compels modern Marxists to reconsider completely their views on the sense of history in the Communist ideal State.

The vulnerability of those, like Hegel and Marx, who did not look beyond man for the goal of history, was clearly perceived by the piercing intellect of Friedrich Nietzsche. If one rejects Christianity and according to this prophet hence renounces the idea of a personal God, one should also have the courage to be consistent and return to the pre-Christian view of history: the cycle, the eternal return of all things. "Who does not believe in a cyclical process of all things must believe in the arbitrary God—this is the unavoidable outcome of my thoughts

59

on this question, contrary to all prevailing theistic thinking!"
(author's translation).[61] It is curious to reflect that Nietzsche
himself balked at its radical consequence and in his *Superman*
assigned a purpose to history all the same. But he saw through
his own logical inconsistency and attempted to find a solution in
the *amor fati*, which makes us feel gratified if we are allowed to
help the wheel of fate revolve.

Such ambiguity may also be observed in the philosophy of
Jean-Paul Sartre. Human existence is basically senseless, both
individually and socially. This position is illustrated by Simone
de Beauvoir in her novel *Tous les Hommes sont mortels* (All
Men Are Mortal), when describing the attempts of Raymond
Fosca, who cannot die, to give sense to his life.[62] Whatever
Fosca may do, however great the energy with which he pursues
his ever-changing ideals, his efforts are ultimately "for nothing," senseless. If behind this desperate view of history we see
modern man in his situation of *Angst* and helplessness, without
a possibility of salvation because he repudiates the Savior and
besides accepts the dialectics of Sartre's philosophy which offer
"proof" of all this—man in his composition of *être-en-soi*
("being-for-itself") is a *passion inutile* ("a useless passion")—
then we must concede that this is a masterly refutation of all
who put the purpose of history in man alone. Whoever does so
fails to provide history with a purpose, all affirmations to the
contrary notwithstanding. He makes it senseless.

Still, this "consistent" refutation is not entirely consistent.
To begin with, time and again Sartre and his followers are illog-
ical when they pronounce a meaningful whole to be meaningless
(as we saw before, we can only speak about history by considering it a meaningful entity). Next, they have no choice but to
follow up their conclusions by stating that such a process, styled
senseless by them, does not even exist! Sartre's philosophy
denies the possibility of continuity, an essential element of a
process: there is no human nature; there is no synthesis of past-

60

present-future in the ever-annihilating *pour-soi*; there is no "other" with whom the making of history is shared. Paradoxically enough, Sartre's man is "unhistorical"; his phenomenology detracts from the reality he wishes to describe.[63] How else can it be explained, in his solution of such senselessness, that a character like Fosca is persistently inspired by an ideal, that he always tries to give a purpose to his life anew? By the fiction of his immortality? How can one explain that men, in the past and present, will go on living, striving upward in spite of all their faults? How can there be room in Sartre's dialectics for man, if man's existence is only possible by the impossible? An individual without a purpose does not act, does not exist. This was better understood by Hegel and Marx, although they placed this purpose where it was unable to function, in man alone.

Little wonder that Sartre, as Nietzsche did, amended his own radical views and has come to accept a purpose for history after all. We must only regret a lack of critical insight here, for in his *Critique de la raison dialectique* he accepts the Marxist interpretation of history dogmatically: "I consider Marxism as the unsurpassable philosophy of our times" (author's translation).[64] He sees Marxism as the authentic expression of the distress and redemption of the proletariat.[65] Against the background of this ultimate purpose of history each particular sense gets its own interpretation.[66] True, Sartre does have serious objections to certain opinions of Marx, Engels, and later Marxists, but this does not touch the basic views with which we are concerned here. One may be pleased that Sartre has abandoned his interpretation of senselessness but at the same time wonder how he means to combine Marxist purposefulness with his own existentialism. Our main objection, finally, is that as soon as the final goal has been reached, it will in its turn appear to be a particular one, requiring another interpretation of history in the Communist ideal State. This means that Sartre can offer no philosophical solution for the phenomenon of history as such.

Karl Jaspers, another existentialist, has attempted to provide a better solution by taking a middle course between purposefulness and purposelessness. His thesis, already referred to in another context, is briefly as follows: (1) Those who speak about the sense, purpose, and unity of history are right. To do so is of vital importance. (2) Those who affirm that this sense, purpose, and unity can never be grasped by us are, however, quite as right.[67]

Sense, purpose, and unity must be present in history, but they can only be so as "limit ideas" (*Grenzvorstellungen*),[68] a belief that is essential but whose content can never be defined. Any fixation is a falsification. One cannot omit it, but one must never lose sight of its relativity. Never is *my* sense of history, as voiced by me, absolute. It is always replaceable and will be replaced in the direction of my point of reference.

> The One is rather the infinitely remote point of reference, which is origin and goal at one and the same time; it is the One of transcendence. As such it cannot be, so to speak, taken captive, it cannot be the exclusive possession of a historical faith that could be enforced upon us as truth *per se*.[69]

But if this is right, Jaspers' middle course is only a delusion. No doubt it is correct to contend that the scientific explanations of various periods in history, or of the sense of one period, can never be definitive. But what of the philosophical sense of history as such? Jaspers' clear dividing line between concept and reality, between our idea of the goal and the real ultimate goal, between the world in which history takes its course and the God who reveals himself in that world in such a way that his revelation can never be unique,[70] and Jaspers' rejection of Christianity on philosophical grounds[71]—all these make it plain that even he remains a relativist. Against his view, as against Sartre's, the objection must be raised that in a way his philosophy is not sufficiently existentialist because he fails to grasp the true phenomenon of history, history *as* history. He comes close to the correct solution, but at the decisive moment he refuses to take the last step, which would open the mind (with all its inadequacy and humility before the mystery) to absolute truth. The transcendence at which he arrives has not at the same time immanence in his philosophy or in history. The reasons for this are not to be found in the phenomenon of history but in Jaspers' Kantian agnostic past, which so far has prevented him from crossing the bridge which he himself built so well in order to get at the truth.

Conclusion

Our conclusions of this brief survey of the development of the "sense of history" itself, may be summarized as follows: as a Christian I see the only solution to be in the revelation given us by Christ; as a philosopher, however, I am not qualified to deal with this revelation in its supernatural aspects, inaccessible as it is to my purely human reason; finally, as a historian I have to accept some facts that are of vital importance to philosophers as well.

First, the Greeks did not reflect on a "sense of history"; nor did any other non-Judeo-Christian thinkers, with the possible exception of Zarathustra in Iran.

Next, Christianity, having had its way prepared by Judaism, broke open the cycle toward the straight line, and history found its fulfillment in the person of Jesus Christ. The manner in which this happened merits theological reflection.

Third, all those who, in the times of the Enlightenment or afterward, considered Christianity outdated and looked for a solution outside the Christian faith (or for one opposed to it) did indeed transfer history to a new sphere of interest. They must be judged, on the other hand, as having failed as philosophers because they would derive unproved postulates from a theology they rejected. From a theological point of view too, they were found to fall short because they rejected, by their a priori, the factual solution in Christ and therefore were unable to keep to the right course.

Finally, my own solution. The argument concluding to the self-realization of man, his growth toward maturity, is not based on unproved postulates but is an entirely philosophical one. Having defined man's purpose more specifically as "the greatest possible likeness to God," our reasoning leaves us in the dark as to where this maximum may be found; but at the same time our reasoning remains open, a thing essential to all Christian philosophy. The solution we cannot find ourselves may be granted us by God. Such an attitude enables us to keep to the right path, our minds illuminated; but the source of light stays hidden to philosophical reason. It is the mysterious light of faith; hence the last word on our theme is with theology, explicitly starting from faith. Theology, however, cannot do its work without philosophy. Pieper emphasizes that asking about the sense of history clearly shows how philosophy cannot do without theology nor theology without philosophy. In point of fact, this interdependence is always and essentially present.[72]

Now Catholics who deny the possibility of a philosophical interpretation of history seem to me to oppose an incorrect view of the task of philosophy rather than the philosophical concept itself.[73] Contrary to what Marrou assumes, there is no need for a philosopher of history to know the whole of history. It is on this erroneous assumption that he bases his rejection of the philosophy of "history as a happening"; but philosophy is not a summation of the results of science. It has its own view of reality, considering being as such and history as such. Sciacca and Malevez cannot endorse without reservation this purpose of philosophy. They repudiate a philosophy of history because philosophy cannot have the final word. I have to admit, of course, that the result of our philosophical argument is not absolute clarity, without darkness or mystery. Like all philosophy, the philosophy of history has to recognize its imperfections and must be open

to faith and theology, to more than human reason can understand. This does not alter the fact that it is this philosophy which
pronounces an ultimate wherefore on the meaning of history,
human existence, because it is within its competence to assert
the existence of God. It is its task to view things in their relation
to God, and there is no compelling motive to declare this task
impossible when dealing with the sense, the meaning, of history.
In our philosophical argument we have not been concerned with
the individual proper, nor is he the object of history, as we shall
see. For this reason Sciacca's objection that there is no philosophy of history because such a philosophy does not touch the
individual, is invalid. Now it would not be at all surprising if
Malevez, Sciacca, and the others who have no use for a philosophy of history unwittingly intended something different
from what they so insistently argue. Might it not be that the
ultimate reason for their attitude is that they have become pain-
fully aware of how hard it is in our time for philosophical reflections on the meaning of life and history to find acceptance?
In fact, the present world situation may cause us to have our
doubts about philosophy's alleged gift of certainty and to wonder whether mankind in its self-realization is still moving toward God. It is a good thing, then, to have something more than
philosophy and to receive an unambiguous answer through one's
faith. It would be wrong, however, to escape into belief if in
this belief we were to reject the certainties of reason. We should
be faced with precisely the same difficulties as those experienced
by Karl Barth, the Protestant theologian, who while refusing to
attribute a purpose to history and while denying that there is
any value to profane events must reconcile this view with the
fact of the Incarnation of the Son of God in the temporal sequence of events. The scope of the present book does not permit
our digressing into the subject of Barth's theology, but we can
at least refer briefly to some Catholic theologians who have been
influenced by him to some extent.

65

At this point I must not omit to deal with another, a purely philosophical point, touching upon the philosophical argument about the meaning of history. There are opponents who deny its stringency, thus relegating the final solution to the Christian faith alone. They may agree with my argument until the sense of history is characterized as the self-realization of man or as man's growth toward adulthood, but it is here that they make their stand. The next step, an indispensable complement—of fathoming this self-realization, this growth, and discovering it as the greatest possible assimilation to God—they cannot take. Man realizing himself they can concede; but man becoming like God, glorifying God, they cannot. And do not think this objection can come only from such atheists as Marxists, according to whom man's self-realization is the only purpose of history. Theists too may raise the objection that man's self-realization is not identical with his similitude to God because man has to determine his purpose in freedom and is therefore capable of going expressly against this pursuit of God. Speaking morally, man can sin, he can persist in his sin, and as a result he can miss his goal.

First, such opponents ought to realize that their objections, if one accepts the fact of human freedom, may also be raised against the self-realization of man. Not only matter, but conversely spirit itself, may be spiritualized. We see this happen in our technical age. The more that spirit, the source of technology, dominates matter, the more it is dominated by technology, so much so as to become its slave. Only a specific, spiritual attitude of free, spiritual, ultimately religious man will be capable of preventing this death of the spirit. In other words, man's self-realization too may develop in various directions. It is possible to become more man or less, according to what standards are used in assessment. Still, it is better, I think, not immediately to introduce moral judgments into ontological considerations about history. I merely intend to present here history's ontological basis, the idea underlying all further history as "made" by free men.

The essential objection, which is that man may miss his final purpose (that is, God), could be countered in the same way. It may be useful, however, to enter into this in some detail, if only to clarify my own point of view. Now if we say that it is possible for the individual human being to miss his purpose by persisting in sinning and thus turning from God, we have to concede this possibility of individual deviation; but this does not prove anything for mankind as a whole. The philosophy of history is concerned with mankind as a whole, and from the fact that some of its individual members may not attain their purpose we must not conclude to the impossibility of this goal for all.

But, one might insist, our philosophical argument started from man as man. True, and that is why we have to supplement and broaden this first and provisional reply. Let us go over our argument again. Like our opponents, we started from the self-realization of man. In order to be real, our argument ran, this realization demanded some goal, some purpose—a purpose, that is, which is not merely immanent, remaining on the human level, but at the same time a purpose that transcends man—namely, his attainment of God. What do I contend here? Not that the human individual, or mankind, must of necessity reach this purpose and cannot deviate from it, but that this purpose of man and mankind must be *capable of being realized* if the reality of self-realization is to be explained. The purpose has to be possible, or the very act will become impossible. To be sure, man can resist this purpose, but even such resistance—in fact, the total deviation at death—is only possible through the existence of purpose. Even in sin man acts in dependence on his divine final cause, and the only reason that he can possess this finite good is that in his deepest being he is directed toward the infinite good.

67

We must therefore distinguish between the *possibility* of the purpose which is affirmed, on one hand, and the *necessity* of definitive attainment which is left open, on the other. Moral categories here are of no concern, but the reality of the purpose is vital. Man realizes himself in history, and imparts sense to it, in numerous ways. Only when history has an end are the interpretations of it—differing according to eras, peoples, and so forth—possible. Man's realization can only be attained through his ultimate direction toward the attainment of God. It is in God that he has his origin. He is the image of God, has God's likeness stamped on him, and even in sin cannot entirely oppose what he is. The final purpose remains present by its real possibility. Philosophy does not tell us any more on this point. It has no opinion about a man who has undoubtedly reached his final goal; it simply does not know and is left with a query to be solved only by theology. Theology informs us through faith that Jesus Christ, the God-man, has definitely reached his final goal by his death, resurrection, and ascension. In him—and, owing to his election, in his Mother as well—the possibility of the purpose has been fulfilled. In the head of mankind, man has attained his purpose and through this has glorified man, who is God. We know through our faith how real the goal of similitude to God is.

The same faith tells us more about the way this goal is reached. For Christ it was the way of the cross. His Church has to bear it also, and only by passion through the catastrophic victory of the antichrist will the body of Christ attain its completion. Here we shall find the ultimate explanation of the togetherness of good and evil in the self-realization of man. Not until we see them in the light of original sin and redemption, of the cross and the resurrection, of Christ and the antichrist, will all things become clear to us.

I intend to refer later on to present-day considerations about these *données* of our faith, but I must digress here to speak about the evolution of humanity, which I have touched on previously.

Progress?

In using the terms *development* and *growth*, I have identified them with the self-realization of man. Experience has taught me, however, that such terminology may cause misunderstanding—and even confusion with the still-living concept of "progress" as the Enlightenment knew it. Moreover, the use of the opposite pair "conservative" and "progressive" is popular, so we can understand that serious historians try to steer clear of such ambiguities. Lucien Febvre, in his *Appendice* to the posthumous work of his friend Marc Bloch, *Apologie pour l'histoire ou métier d'historien*, refrains from judging Bloch's ideas about history except for this: "I only wish to make one remark. Nowhere in the present book, if I am not mistaken, does the word *evolution* occur" (author's translation).[74]

Such a negative reaction is understandable. To many people, words like *development* and *growth* are synonymous with the naïve meaning of "continuous progress," as understood by the philosophers of the Enlightenment. Now the first question is whether we are right in associating the idea of progress with *the* philosophers of the eighteenth century. On paying close attention to those philosophers we shall discover many different shades in their views of this idea. Karl Löwith significantly entitles his chapter on the philosophy of this period "Progress versus Providence."[75] Quoting John B. Bury he shows how the decline in the belief in Providence and the rise of the idea of progress were closely linked: "It was not till men felt independent of Providence that they could organize a theory of progress."[76] Löwith demonstrates this clearly in his discussion of such men as Proudhon, Comte, Condorcet, Turgot, and Voltaire (note that Löwith's book is composed "regressively"; that is, looking from the present toward the past), but it should be noticed that this rejection of Providence took place in stages. Kant, for instance, from the very assumption of the continuous progress of the human race, concluded to the judicious guidance of Providence.[77] Fichte did not consider his time to be the best; on the contrary, he spoke of the arrival at a "condition of complete sinfulness" (author's translation).[78] Hegel, as we have seen earlier, saw the development of humanity (a secularization of the Christian idea of final time) as occurring within a period identical with his own time. For the typical seventeenth- and eighteenth-century rationalists, however, as Löwith rightly observes, time did not arrive at its fulfillment, but could go on and on.[79] We could give, as Rothacker does,[80] a lengthy historical exposition devoted to this idea of development, discovering numerous Christian, religious, antireligious, and other shades in it, but we should finally arrive at the conclusion that in the eighteenth century an idea of progress presented itself which in various guises came to life with all these philosophers. A good, rather-more-critical formula was given by W. Krug in his *Allgemeines Handwörterbuch der philosophischen Wissenschaften* (General Dictionary of Philosophical Sciences) of 1827. He spoke of *Fortschritt* ("progress") as of a "gradual perfection of humanity." Not everyone was in agreement with this idea, Krug said, because people assume that a culture manifests a continuous cyclical course of rise and decline, a view which Krug thought was partly right.

> But as a whole, humanity, like all the world, is subject to the general rule of evolution, by which all things are in progress . . . Hence mankind nowadays is incontestably on a higher level than in any former time, extensively as well as intensively. Mankind has made progress, is capable of more, and cannot but progress because at no time can we say that the human race is as it is bound to be according to the imperative claims of reason. [Author's translation.][81]

Those who believe in the guidance of God are, additionally, convinced that under his guidance we are always progressing intellectually and morally, each of us being obliged to contribute to the best of his ability.

The idea of progress has captured man's mind to such an extent that after all kinds of philosophical opposition, after our sad experience of impending and actual war, concentration camps, and other atrocities, we still may read in the 1946 edition of the Encyclopedia Americana under the entry "Progress," showing less caution and critical sense than Krug exhibited in 1827:

> *Progress,* the advancement of the world, moral, mental and material as exhibited in history. Physical science, which has so recently demonstrated the gradual improvement of material types in the animal and vegetable world, has compelled metaphysical speculation to conform its general principles to the axioms formulated by physical observation and experiment.

The physical law of progress, here termed *meliorism,* is alleged to rule in all spheres. *Meliorism* (from the Latin *melior,* "better") is explained thus: "Meliorism embodies the truth that as far as human experience and observation can extend there has been improvement in things, progress in the universe, advancement in the world. Pessimism becomes a contradiction in terms." Naturalists, historians, sociologists—all will declare that in the past the condition of plants, animals, people, and human institutions was worse. "Meliorism is the doctrine of the positivist, because it is no metaphysical system which interprets facts by an a priori assumption: it is simply an induction from a summary of . . . facts."

I apologize for these lengthy quotations,[82] but it seemed wise to confront the reader with authentic views: Krug's as a good synopsis of the ideas of his time, and the one from the Encyclopedia Americana as a sign that even after two world wars in our century positivism still retains its dogmatic followers. In addition, both texts clearly indicate the reasons that the idea of such continuous world improvement is accepted. Facts compel thinking man to recognize an evolution, in a progressive sense, in all fields. "In man, as in all the world," Krug had it. The encyclopedia puts it the other way around: in the physical world and hence in man. Against an argument based on "facts" we must proceed carefully. Undoubtedly there are facts which, in our eyes too, stand for progress, but against them we witness a considerable number of facts showing decline. Krug concedes this; the American author does not. To the latter's abolition of slavery, mentioned as an instance of progress, we can unfortunately oppose the reintroduction of slavery in the Nazi concentration camps, which in 1946 ought to have been known to him. In history, facts are rallied around a focal point. Otherwise the mass of facts from the past will remain without shape, without utterance, and certainly without conclusive proof. Rejecting any a priori, the anonymous American writer to whom we have been referring nevertheless speaks of an

> induction from a summary of those facts which physical science has most recently set forth as the proud result of the newest, the most unbiased, and the most incontrovertible deductions from experiment and observation, in the whole world of material, social and political phenomena.[83]

This presupposes something more than mere facts; "induction from a summary" and even "deduction" are spoken of, but one thing, as in the first quotation about progress, stands out: the evidence rests with science, which manifests the same evolution in all spheres. The same equation, although not so obvious, is found with Krug; and it is here, not in the facts, that we must look for the *raison d'être* of meliorism. If such concepts as progress and evolution are applied in exactly the same way to both history and biology, they are considered univocal. These quotations show only two examples of this characteristic feature of the philosophy of progress, which on observing some particular development in the realm of biology, for example, is apt to transpose offhand such a biological notion to psychology or history. But this is a scientific error which undermines all arguing from the facts. Of course it is often permissible, and sometimes unavoidable, to employ concepts derived from one discipline in another. In our case, we may safely use the idea of evolution, undoubtedly biological in its origin, in psychology or history— but not until carefully looking into the interrelation of their objects. And here we can justifiably borrow the words of Lange-veld on the subject:

> Adoption of notions is possible, on condition that the adopted no-tion is explicitly defined, if the object of the adopting science comprises less and is less general—or better, has greater specific definiteness—as compared to the science from which the notion is taken. Biological sciences occupy themselves with living orga-nisms as such; psychology defines itself to these living organisms not as living beings—this quality is in psychology presupposed as the more general—but as beings with a *behaviour* and insofar as they testify a behaviour. [Italics in original.][84]

In fact, the living being which is man will show evolution, but in psychology this concept is to be specified in accordance with its object, and history must do the same if it wishes to consider man in its specific way. As Romein negatively put it, we must "de-biologize" the biological concept.[85]

But all this does not occur until later. First we must ask whether the biological concept itself is correct. A layman might be inclined to take this for granted, but on consulting biologists he would learn that the biological concept of growth is by no means a "simple continuous development" of some plant or animal. Such a process happens in discontinuity as well. Thus the pruning of a fruit tree will stimulate a spurt of growth, the apparent regression in reality causing more progress and pro-ducing more fruit.

When, furthermore, we apply this biological concept of de-velopment to the theory of evolution, we see that there too biol-ogists have come to be much more prudent than in the naïve enthusiasm of the early days. One modern view, as advocated by Teilhard de Chardin, is given in Delfgaauw's synopsis:

> Evolution does not necessarily stand for direct progress along the same line. It may shift from one line to another. The ascending evolution from lower to higher beings is progress. Cosmically, progress stands for greater complexity in corpuscular structure; from a life point of view, for an increase of vital consciousness; humanely seen, for more freedom. [Author's translation.][86]

Therefore it will be necessary for us to distinguish in the naïve idea of progress the biological, psychological, and historical concepts, and the subdivisions which each allows according to its object. Hence also, the idea of progress in history, which is our immediate concern, will be differentiated according to its various sectors. The history of economics, of politics, of civilization, and of the Church—each presents a development in accordance with that particular sphere. If, for instance, we hear of Romein's definition of evolution as "changes determined by changes in human relations,"[87] this may sound quite plausible in its generality; but the context makes it clear that to him the socioeconomic factors are the key to these changes, and one single evolutionary concept—namely, the one pertaining to economics—has been interpreted here as *the* evolutionary concept of history. True, the socioeconomic aspect doubtless does have its importance in all spheres of history—and thanks to Marx the importance of this truth is growing upon us—but it would show a one-sided cast of mind to allow the evolutionary aspect of history as such to be determined by this single aspect. Romein's definition does not sufficiently emphasize the importance of the free, spiritual element. Accordingly, it is inadequate for the evolution in other areas, especially in the history of civilization or of the Church.

At the moment, however, it must be my first task to enlarge upon this concept of evolution, a term I have already used occasionally when dealing with the philosophy of history where history in general was indicated as the self-realization of man to be identified with the growth or evolution toward maturity. What are we to understand here by this concept of growth, of evolution, of self-realization? What specification is imparted to the concept which covers its being equated with the self-realization of man?

The answer can be brief because I need only refer to the previous philosophical exposition, its point being that mankind is realizing itself in its numerous human beings and thus is directed toward the purpose of this realization. It cannot be otherwise because the spirit, by virtue of its essence, always attempts to transcend its limitation. To be itself it cannot be contained in itself but must surrender to other than itself. Therefore it realizes itself in matter, the alienation of the spirit. This happens in a permanent succession of acts. Its being is becoming, its reality realization. Insofar as this self-realization takes place continuously in individuals as well as in the whole of mankind; insofar as there is always an alienation of the spirit in matter by the spirit's reflections, actions, and work, by its doings in the widest sense of the word; insofar as we may speak here of a "process," in the original Latin sense of "going farther"— in the same way we may speak of "growth," insofar as the spirit, on its long journey through time, has come to express itself more and more in matter. The concept of evolution, if subject to the same restrictions, may be used in the same way; that is, we must not interpret it as an unfolding of some reality that is completely present but as the one human spirit realizing itself further and further in our many realizations.

Now, do *growth* and *evolution* stand for progress here? Is mankind really always advancing? Our metaphysical argument does not provide us with a direct answer on this point, but the alienation of the spirit may be found both as a spiritualization of matter and as a materialization of the spirit, depending upon man's free choice. Here we are entering the domain of ethics, where judgment is given according to moral, meta-historical standards. According to such standards, progress on the road toward freedom is found in the abolition of slavery (the view of the Encyclopedia Americana), decline in the twentieth-century concentration camps and forced labor of the innocent; progress in the abolition of polygamy, decline in the increasing number of divorce cases; progress, generally speaking, in the sensitivity of the world conscience to human values (the great improvement of our day), but at the same time decline in the threat of a nuclear war's destroying all such values; in genocide, of which the mass murder of six million Jews is but one example; in the lack of respect for human life which shows itself in euthanasia, abortion, and so forth.[88]

In this way we have arrived at various sectors of history, all demanding a further specification of our general concept of evolution according to the nature of the sector and the standard applied. Thus we can see, with Romein, progress in the realm of technology, where the qualifications of "higher" and "better" are only applied on the basis of the power of production to oust a previous stage. Romein's examples from military history clearly demonstrate that progress did not proceed in a straight line but from a backward, hazardous level of life toward a more elevated one. The more advanced someone is, the more backward he will become.

One more example in another sphere by the same author: years ago the catalog of the British Museum was renowned over those of a great many libraries, but later it was considered lagging behind the printed ones of smaller collections because it was handwritten.[89] Britain, once preeminently forward, presents us with numerous other examples of Romein's law, which for that matter is in the same line as Toynbee's law of challenge and response, according to which conditions should not be easy for civilization. The stress of adversity stimulates it to response, causing it to overcome its difficulties and make progress.

As regards a detailed specification of the notion of evolution in the various areas of history, here too we should beware of a univocal concept. Although Romein's exposition is very skillful and subtle, it still would appear that his attempts to find some law of progress in history tend to go toward such univocality, which is seen by him as an ideal. The only correct way to handle the concepts of evolution and progress in history is through analogy, wherein instead of being guided by some a priori we consider the evolution according to the diverse planes of historical reality on which it is taking place. If the plane, the sector, be different, so will be the way of the evolution. In a material area, progress will be obvious because on this particular plane the aspect of change manifests itself clearly. On the other hand, should a spiritual atmosphere prevail, then it will be a great deal more difficult to discern the aspect of progress, the obvious reason being that on this level the aspect of permanence is predominant.

A few examples may be helpful to illustrate my line of thought. In the field of military technology man has made enormous progress. He has invented the nuclear bomb (I am not speaking here about the humane or moral disadvantages of the bomb but merely of its technical aspects). Whereas spear and shield as weapons of warfare are in our civilization things of the past, to Plato's contemporaries they were implements of the highest caliber. A univocal interpretation of progress would tend to reject Plato's philosophy as old-fashioned for the same spear-and-shield reasons. No doubt there are some transitory aspects in Plato's dialogues. On the other hand, the aspect of permanence prevails so much in his philosophy that even now we are attracted by his works; we attempt to rethink his thoughts and prefer him to many a less brilliant philosopher of our times. The reason has nothing to do with his belonging to the spear-and-shield era but is simply that the actuality of his philosophy, even in our nuclear era, enables us to be Platonists now.

Such transcendence of their times is also met in other truly great philosophers whose influence reaches far beyond their own day. We must not, of course, overlook the fact that even the best of them could only pursue their philosophy by starting from their own experience. Hence one's experience within a particular life-span is at the same time a help and a limitation. Permanence does not imply a static, closed system, immutably valid for all times. The philosophy of the Angelic Doctor was decidedly not that of an angel, seeing that his philosophy too had to contain some aspect of human progress in order to be true philosophy. But the concept of progress used to indicate the evolution of thirteenth-century Thomism toward twentieth-century neo-Thomism is essentially different from the concept of material progress. In the spiritual sphere it is the aspect of permanence that prevails. We ought to realize, though, that the vital character of this permanence goes back to the fact that, in Aristotle's words, "the act of the intellect is life" (author's translation).[90]

A third example, on the religious-spiritual level, may be even more striking. The Benedictine Order dates back from the beginning of the sixth century, but we cannot very well hold that its spirituality has become outmoded by the foundation of the orders of the Franciscans and Dominicans in the thirteenth century, of the Jesuits in the sixteenth century, and of the secular institutes in the twentieth century. Since Benedict's time changes have occurred in the Benedictine monasteries, of course, as regards nutrition, dress, and so forth, changes geared to different countries and times. There may even have been some adjustment in the original conception of spirituality, but still the aspect of permanence has predominated, and hence a great many twentieth-century Christians—monks, nuns, laymen—find their way to God by living according to the spirit of St. Benedict.

The more spiritual the sphere of history, the more difficult will it be to denote the relevant concept of evolution: the various planes are likely to be confused. On the material plane, progress consists in surpassing—that is, in making superfluous—the previous phase. On the intellectual and spiritual levels, this possibility is also open to lesser gods, less given to thought and spirituality; but at such levels the aspect of permanence is prevalent all the same. This implies, however, that here history becomes more complicated, the concept of progress displaying finer shades. It is not easy to point to a form of progress without reflecting at the same time upon some particular manifestation of decline. I have already referred to this when dealing with the naïve thesis of progress in the Encyclopedia Americana. In fact, a historian cannot hope to know the inner warp and woof characteristics of history, unless they have been revealed to him by God or man—and even then their implications, insofar as they are primarily spiritual, can only be guessed at. From his philosophy of history the historian only knows that evolution will continue until man has reached the greatest possible likeness to God, but it will not be given to him, as a philosopher, to know exactly how and whither that point is attained. He knows there is progress, insofar as things are advancing toward the final purpose, but it seems impossible to me that he should be capable of indicating unerringly merely from the vantage point of his philosophy an absolute progress in man's self-realization.

As a result of the Christian faith, the historian's knowledge is indeed enlarged, and he is enabled to clarify the previous vagueness of the final purpose. But even his theological knowledge is necessarily found wanting if he should wish to know God's unrevealed intentions at a specific moment of history or if he should ask about any intellectual and religious progress we may have made since the Middle Ages. The tenets of his faith only confirm for the historian the extreme complexity of his subject. As I pointed out before, we know on one hand that the fullness of history has reached us with Christ's cross, resurrection, and ascension; but human happenings have not come to a standstill, on the other hand. Though Christ has been victorious over the senselessness of the world of sin, the completion of the work so begun is left to his members. Christ's body has to be extended. Man's self-realization now comes to signify the growth of Christ in us, a growth to continue until he comes. We are living in the period of eager tension between his first and second coming. Hence evolution, progress even, is essential here. But it will be attended by (apparent) decline, insofar as for the Church of Christ, as for Christ himself, the road of the cross is an essential condition of arriving at the Resurrection. The theologian in the historian will doubtless help him to see all human events in the right perspective— namely, that of God—but still the historian hesitates to employ this light of mystery in spheres where it does not appear as such, is invisible, where resorting to it could degrade it, humanly speaking. Such simplification would do injustice to the complexities of reality, for instance when man's self-realization is completely absorbed by his becoming a Christian or the reverse. Living as we do between the first and the second coming, we do not essentially possess the complete identity between self-realization and becoming a Christian because we have not yet arrived, because it has not been revealed yet what we shall be; our place is in the distinction between ecclesiastical history and profane history.

Ecclesiastical history deals with the growth of a human community *insofar as it is a community in Christ*, a religious one. Profane history covers the growth of a human community *insofar as it is a community of men*, serving members in mundane, temporal, natural aspects. This distinction is a matter of experience. Poetry, politics, sports, technology—all these are different from religion. But this is also taught us by faith. Man's self-realization does not come to a stop when God becomes man; it is only then that it attains its full significance. A supernaturalism that drowns the profane in the religious is

80

unreal, unchristian. Man's nature is not destroyed by Christ but incorporated, redeemed, entirely realized, "For the Son of Man came to seek and to save what was lost" (Luke 19:10). This is what enabled us to provide a philosophical argument for the necessity of man's self-realization, and this argument is by no means made void now that the full light of the faith allows us to discover quite new dimensions in it. However, when it comes to discerning or discussing possible progress in the religious realm, a good deal of circumspection is called for. Reality is not simple enough for a naïve observation of progress.

The meaning of our life on earth

To prevent, or perhaps correct, any misunderstanding, let it be said at once that in expressing an attitude of reserve toward it I do not wish to imply that there is no such thing as progress; nor, where it does exist, do I mean that we should not contribute to it with all our might. The only point I wish to make is that this progress, so obviously verifiable in the material world, is analogously present in the more spiritual spheres, where, however, we are not supplied with such easy proofs because the spiritual realm has a permanent aspect and because progress is closely linked with decline. In order to be more clear it may be useful to go a little further into the question arising from the present context, What is the relation between profane history and ecclesiastical history? More exactly, What significance has our life on earth, in a specific sense, for the end of time? What is the meaning of the concern modern Christians have with the profane life of these days? What is the point in their work, in the care of their family and country, in their interest in a united Europe, one world, better international relations, to enable them to attain such ideals? Though this matter is primarily theological, in a philosophy of history it must at least be considered. I shall therefore deal with it briefly and refer interested readers to special publications for details.

81

Theologians who in the past fifteen years especially have been considering this problem—two world wars within half a century are surely sufficient grounds for its investigation—have provided us with two extreme positions, between which lie numerous more moderate variants. Somewhat crudely formulated, these are the transcendental, or eschatological, and the immanent, or incarnational, schools of thought. The first holds that because Christ came to this earth and will come again, all human activities in the interim are insignificant. The second says that because Christ came to this earth and will come again, all human activities in the interim are of the utmost importance, inasmuch as they contribute to the building up of Christ's kingdom.

Let us examine these theological reflections on the Catholic doctrine that the incarnation of the Son of God, his life, crucifixion, and resurrection have given a meaning to history.

In 1950 Marcel Moré, then editor of *Dieu Vivant*, an influential theological-philosophical monthly, gave in an obituary notice of the French Christian philosopher Emmanuel Mounier a good résumé of the eschatological trend:

> neither morals nor the "spiritual" in the immanent sense in which this word is too widely understood, could have the slightest perceptible effect on the evolution of society. The world of enslavement and of the destruction of man could not be fought by a more sophisticated, more subtle technique; the only way to break it is by the invasion, in the visible world, of an invisible world which has its roots in Transcendence: the world of the Poor and of the eternal Beggar, of eschatological Holiness, that of the Living God and of the Living Church. [Author's translation.][91]

In other words, Moré holds that it is impossible to improve this world at all. We are caught in the inescapable grip of a technologic-economic process which, as we learn from history, follows its inexorable course. We must not take our stand in it for we should perish in doing so. The only solution will come from above, through a rift in this world process, through the working of the invisible world as it is present in the suffering

82

servant of Yahweh, in eschatological saintliness, in the church of the catacombs. The relation between the sacred and the profane is merely vertical; the shape of this world must pass, this being its sense.

In other authors we find world history representing the very empire of darkness, essentially opposed to the realm of grace. The Christian does take his place in this world, but he has no share in its history. His life consists in renouncing the world, doing good to his fellowmen, earning his livelihood, while waiting for the Lord. While repudiating such an attitude as being radical, some people will make a distinction resulting in a difference: the Christian does not participate in world history as a Christian, but he does so as a human being. For some Catholics and Protestants this separation between church and world has to serve as an argument in favor of a breakthrough in politics, founded on the dualism of the kingdom of God and that of this world which prevents the latter from being Christianized. The vision of history shared by a good many Reformationists is broadly based on this interpretation of a vertical relationship between God and the world, on stressing a transcendence in which God's intervention is no more than incidental (as in the case of the Incarnation), not enduringly transforming.

The incarnational view of the theology of history does not deny that there is a disproportion between our work on earth and that in the new heaven and earth, but at the same time it affirms a certain continuity. The second coming calls for the action of man, not his repression, for Christian activity is already sharing in the grace of the Word's having become flesh, and by virtue of the Spirit this life of grace also has its impact on bodily and earthly things. The coming of Christ is grace from above, but

> eternity is a fruit whose blossom would be the present time. Without the gift of a radiant summer which descends from heaven there would not be any autumnal ripeness, but still it is not less

83

true that the ripe fruit is set and developed in the flowering of spring. [Author's translation.][92]

The number of places in Scripture supporting this point of view is considerably smaller than eschatologists can quote in support of their opinion. I have already mentioned Paul's words about completing Christ's body, about the fullness of time—texts that by their nature bear primarily on the kingdom of God in its aspect of grace. Nevertheless, it should be added at once that Scripture does not know a setting apart of the spiritual nature of man (for which the above would be valid), excluding his body as well as the world. On the contrary, all of man, the whole world, is to be redeemed. The body of man is the shrine of the Holy Ghost and a member of Christ, and by eating the Body of the risen Christ a Christian receives his resurrection and immortality. "Therefore, whether you eat or drink, or do anything else, do all for the glory of God" (1 Corinthians 10:31). Thus the profane will be integrated into the religious. In this respect we often find quoted "Be fruitful and multiply; fill the earth and subdue it . . ." (Genesis 1:28). Catholic theology, though, need not limit itself to arguments from Scripture; accordingly, advocates of the incarnational view adduce other proofs, derived above all from the fact of the Incarnation, the resulting influence of the divine life in the Son on his humanity, and because he is its Head, on all mankind, including corporality and the world. Catholic theology teaches that the grace of Paradise had its repercussions on bodily things in the same way as the Fall has entailed disharmony in man himself and in the world.

Another argument, taken by Malevez from history, is that progress in specifically human things has occurred preeminently in Europe, the region most influenced by Christianity.[93] His fellow Jesuit Teilhard de Chardin advances a much more detailed scientific argument, which rests, however, on a pronounced bias toward the incarnational view of history. Teilhard de Chardin sees the whole universe in biological evolution toward man, and man in his turn toward the society of men which is associated with the God-man. This evolution is continuous in its discontinuity, presenting such jumps as from the subhuman toward the human, from nature toward grace, from the present world toward the other.[94]

M. I. Montuclard, also writing in French, holds that already in profane history a mysterious redemption of man by man is taking place, by which unbelievers, in their way, are working for the same salvation as are the faithful, thus receiving a redemption which is in fact Christian. It will be the task of the Church in her work of salvation to adapt herself as much as possible to the Marxist hope of salvation.[95]

Having been presented with an outline of these two opposing views, the reader is entitled to the author's opinion of them. Let me, then, first stress the point that a Catholic solution of this problem should always include both aspects, incarnational as well as eschatological. I may stress one more than the other, but the aspect of Incarnation in itself, without the cleavage owing to the unexpected intervention from above, or an eschatological view denying the presence of the kingdom of God *now*, will have to be rejected. This approach may seem more reasoned if we turn to a particular example, of how opposing facts lend themselves to an essential association in the life of the Church.

In the Catholic Church marriage is a sacrament. On the other hand, we hear that in the same Church God-devoted celibacy is considered a higher state of life than marriage. In marriage earthly love, the highest specifically human love, is made part of divine worship through sacrament, presenting us with an image of Christ's love for his Bride: Christ loves his Church as a husband loves his wife. Thus Catholic marriage is a clear example of the incarnational aspect in the life of the Church. Beside marriage, however, is celibacy, anticipating the parousia, the new heaven and the new earth, where there is no marrying nor giving in marriage (Matthew 22:30). In fact, religious celibacy represents a belonging body and soul to Christ alone. Here the image of marriage has become reality. By renouncing the goods of this world for Christ's sake man is directed toward a new earth, or rather this new earth is being made here and now, final time having begun already. Seen in this light, celibacy is a clear sign of eschatology in the Church.

More examples could be given, all of them showing that we are in the final days, during which we pray for the coming of the Lord. This earth is important, and yet its shape will pass. How is it, then, that two solutions of contemporary theologians can sometimes be diametrically opposed, hardly leaving room for the contrary thesis? If I may hazard a guess in this difficult matter, I feel the problem goes back to a twofold deficiency in some theologians: lack of a sound philosophical foundation for theological reflection, and inadequate confrontation of their personal opinions with the relevant ecclesiastical documents. Both shortcomings are excusable, seeing that in those circles the theology of history is usually approached via Marxist or Protestant writings. As a rule, Protestant authors are not particularly keen about a philosophical answer; nor are they, understandably, very much interested in documents presenting the teachings of the Catholic Church. On the other hand, because of their specialization Catholic theologians have not always kept abreast of present-day philosophy. The answers to Marxists or existentialists tend to be completely theological but are not based on consultation of their colleagues the philosophers. A theological response is, of course, ultimately necessary; but a true dialogue can only be engaged in on a common, philosophical ground. If these theological shortcomings can be remedied we may have good hopes of arriving at a genuine Catholic solution.

We may find an outline of such a synthesis, on the level of local ecclesiastical authority, in Cardinal Suhard's well-known "Three Letters" whose writer repeatedly referred to Pope Pius

XII and whose advisors were certainly not unacquainted with philosophy. My personal opinion is that a theological answer concerning the appreciation of things terrestrial ought to be sought in this direction. What to me is of particular weight in this matter is the program of Pius XI toward "The Peace of Christ in the Realm of Christ," continued explicitly by Pius XII; subscribed to by John XXIII, and deepened by the Second Vatican Council's Constitution on the Church in the Modern World. In 1925 Pius XI gave his encyclical letter *Quas Primas*, on Christ the King, in which the relationship between things profane and sacral was dealt with. Opposing the laicizing tendencies of his time, Pius XI put forward the idea of the kingship of Christ, Christ as the ruler over our earth. Christ ought to be king not only of the hearts of men but also in public life. In all our private actions, in the life of nations, industry, and labor—in short, in any human environment where man works and lives—he ought positively to be acknowledged as the supreme authority. Laicization is to be cured by Christianization; that is, the profane values will benefit by their integration with religious ones.

Now this does not stand for supernaturalism, theocracy, or clericalism. Here Christ reigns as king, not as priest. His sovereignty will be realized especially by the laymen (Pope Pius XI was the pope of Catholic Action), who are to be autonomous in their own domain. But such autonomy is never absolute; it always goes hand in hand with heteronomy. Man fully and with all his heart applies himself to the realization of earthly values, fulfilling God's mandate for self-realization, but this self-realization is directed toward deification in Christ. Thus we get a good idea of the Catholic view of history, as dealt with in the preceding philosophical argument; namely, the coexistence of continuity and discontinuity.

Man's self-realization is continued in accordance with his essential activities in this world, but Christians know that they will never be able to realize their aim by their own efforts. Here grace from above is indispensable. Therefore, the Church will always consider the secular values essential and will integrate them with the religious. Salvation is, was, and always will be from the Jews. It is an unchangeable fact that Greco-Roman forms have given something to the Church, as is evident in her dogmatic formulations, for example. But never will the Church identify herself with one nation (Israel) or with one philosophy or civilization (Hellenism). *Civilizations are the garments of the Church, which she puts on and takes off,*[96] does not make sufficiently clear, however, that in this contact between the Church and the world there will always remain something of a permanent character, giving evidence that the profane world is joining us on our journey toward finality. In a similar way we see the results of Redemption in the secular world. The influence of Christianity has brought about the recognition and realization of certain general values, such as the dignity of the human person, the equality of men as regards their nature, origin, and destination, and the meaning of history.

The Christian engaged in realizing the profane values may occasionally ask himself whether his work is of any use to him as a Christian. In my opinion the answer to this question must be that insofar as such values of technology, culture, and so forth, are focused on the self-realization of man, such self-realization may awaken in mankind an even greater longing for the end of time. Ambivalence remains: we cannot create the new heaven or the new earth; but an improved condition of man is decidedly a more suitable disposition for them than poverty, war, illness, or lack of development. No doubt it is also possible for God to speak his word when humanity is in the extremes of poverty or in the chaos of war, but it will stand an even slighter chance of being understood in such a situation than when our human condition has improved. Therefore it should be the task of the Christian to work for a better world while being aware that even in case of setbacks, human failure, antagonism by the Evil One, God will continue his work. Redemption comes through the cross; the continuation of that redemption in the Church and in the world occurs in the same way. We know that the shape of this world will pass away. For this reason, in all Christian work a certain detachment is indispensable. We know a humanism of the cross, but at the same time we are fully humanist because the Crucifixion was followed by the Resurrection.

It is Catholic doctrine that this same body of ours shall rise from the dead in a glorified state. Hence for our theme the conclusion would seem to be justified that the new heaven and earth shall have their shapes determined by the age-old work of mankind, unpredictably transformed by the Lord of history. Dominican Père Yves Congar illustrates this felicitously.

> A teacher sets a pupil a series of very difficult problems. The pupil is unable to find the solution, although he comes very near to it and multiplies his efforts. The solution will be given him by the teacher but only when, through all his efforts, the pupil has developed his mind and his powers in a manner that he would not even have dreamt of if the solution had been told him at once. Thus the pupil, in a way, will have elevated himself to the level of the solution; he will receive it only because he has been extended to its measure. [Author's translation.][97]

We may view similarly the relationship between our present earth and the new heaven and new earth. The latter are presented to us by God, from above, but by its activities humanity has made the earth ripe for radical transformation and through God's grace has enabled itself to receive this gift of God.

If this is the Catholic vision of history, we Catholics cannot admit, I think, that we are devoid of ideals in this life, in this world. Together with all people of good will, we possess the ideal of aiming at a better world, but it is ours for time and eternity. What is at stake on this earth is a strange, a miraculous, challenge to create a new heaven as well as a new earth.

HISTORY AS A SCIENCE

The actual philosophical discussion about history as a happening compelled me at the end of the lengthy previous chapter to make an excursion into the field of theology. Returning to our former realm, we shall now attempt to find a philosophical answer to our second major problem, history as a science.

We can call history a science in the truest sense when the human spirit considers itself insofar as it realizes itself in matter, when it grows in adultness insofar as it becomes man and so develops toward the fullness of Christ, all the while reflecting on this happening, on this history as a happening—then and only then.

History as a happening is its supposition, its ontological substratum. Because he is a historical being, man will arrive at the science of history. I have pointed out, with Jaspers, that it took man some time to enter the era of history. A certain cultural level was essential before man could consciously reflect on his existence in the past other than by way of myths and sagas, before he could arrive at history in the full sense of the word, at history as a science. Even then it took history eons to move from the temple of the Muses to her own profane realm, as we have seen.

This, however, is the moment when we must decide whether it is right to call history a science.

Is history a science?

The answer of John Bagnell Bury (1861-1927), in his celebrated Cambridge inaugural lecture, "The Science of History," was, "It has not yet become superfluous to insist that history is a science, no less and no more."[1] The reason for this, he continued, was that only in the nineteenth century did history acquire full scientific status; moreover, even scholars acknowledging this transformation of history were hesitant to accept the consequences. History is not a branch of literature; it has to confine itself to the world of facts by truly objective research so that there will no longer be any different schools of history.

Previous to Bury, Thomas Buckle (1821-1862) had emphasized even more strongly the scientific aspect. His attitude is reflected in the epitome of the first chapter of *General Introduction to the History of Civilization in England*:

> Statement of the resources for investigating history, and proofs of regularity of human actions—These actions are governed by mental and physical laws; therefore both sets of laws must be studied, and there can be no history without natural sciences.[2]

What this implies may become clear from another quotation, which leaves no doubt about Buckle's view.

It is now known that marriages bear a fixed and definite relation to the price of corn; and in England the experience of a century has proved that, instead of having any connexion with personal feelings, they are simply regulated by the average earnings of the great mass of the people: so that this immense social and religious institution is not only swayed, but is completely controlled, by the price of food and by the rate of wages.[3]

Elsewhere, on the continent of Europe, we find the same scientific trend; especially in Germany, where in the preface of the first issue of the *Historische Zeitschrift* (1859) Heinrich von Sybel, its founder, stated in unambiguous terms:

The present review aims, above all, to be a scientific one. Its first task, therefore, should be to represent the true method of historical research and to signal any deviations. . . . This point of view precludes any feudalism, imposing atrophied elements on progressing life; any radicalism, substituting subjective arbitrariness for organic development; any ultramontanism, subjecting natural and spiritual evolution to the authority of the extraneous Church. [Author's translation.][4]

Such extreme views, although voiced by representative historians, will automatically raise opposite ones. Thus we have Bury's successor at Cambridge, Harold W. V. Temperley (1879-1939), saying "In my own memory the idea that history is a science has perished."[5] This outspoken statement against Bury was made in 1930 but had been anticipated as early as 1903 by George Macaulay Trevelyan, grandnephew of Thomas Babington Macaulay. Trevelyan, early in his own famous career, defended in "Clio, a Muse" such historians as his granduncle and Carlyle against the charge, of Bury and other representatives of the "scientific" school, of being no more than charlatans:

The idea that the facts of history are of value as part of an exact science confined to specialists is due to a misapplication of the analogy of physical science . . . history cannot, like physical science, deduce causal laws of general application. . . . The law

92

of gravitation may be scientifically proved because it is universal and simple. But the historical law that starvation brings on revolt is not proved; indeed the opposite statement, that starvation leads to abject submission, is equally true in the light of past events. . . . How indeed could history be a "science"? You can dissect the body of a man, and argue thence the general structure of the bodies of other men. But you cannot dissect a mind; and if you could, you could not argue thence about other minds. . . . I conclude, therefore, that the analogy of physical science has misled many historians during the last thirty years right away from the truth about their profession.[6]

On the other hand, Trevelyan does not deny all scientific aspects of history. On the contrary: "To my mind, there are three distinct functions of history, that we may call the *scientific*, the *imaginative* or *speculative*, and the *literary*" (italics in original).[7] This shows that the author does not belong to one of the two extremist factions among historians, and from the words of the historians themselves the point of this argument will be clear to us. History must not be the mere telling of an interesting tale; it ought to have an accountable knowledge of the past. Surely we will concede this, provided that it is allowed to be itself and is not deformed by being identified with the natural sciences. In other words, Trevelyan is making a stand against the univocal use of the terms *science* and *scientific method*. To many, indeed, there is only one kind of scholarly discipline and one kind of disciplinary method: that of positive science and its way to arrive at the truth. How far this one-sided view has advanced we may infer from the fact that both in the English and French languages the word *science* is now virtually identical with *positive science*. Of course this equation is easily explained by the fact that the positive sciences are the older ones, that they excel by their lucid and exact method, and are more spectacular by their applications, whether these are nuclear bombs or journeys into space. Nevertheless it might be that there exists a different sort of science, one whose results are admittedly less spectacular but would deserve the name of "science" for all that. If so, the answer to the question whether history is a science will depend on our ideas about science. And it is here (having, in accordance with our scheme, first lent our ears to the historians) that we arrive at the philosophy of history as a branch of learning.

In the preceding brief historical sketch of this field I have already drawn your attention to Giovanni Battista Vico,[8] who stressed the duality of learning: the disciplines dealing with nature and those occupying themselves with things human. His contemporaries, however, were too enraptured by the splendid results of the natural sciences to pay attention to his words. Not until historical sense asserted itself in the nineteenth century and the great historians gained influence in wider circles, could men like Dilthey, Windelband, and Rickert start their pioneer work. They laid the foundations for the philosophical distinction between the natural sciences and the *Geisteswissenschaften*[9] ("the sciences of the mind" or "the human studies"). Incidentally, it is quite apparent that we owe to Schiel, the German translator of John Stuart Mill, his explanation of Mill's term *moral sciences.*

Doubtless the thesis of this difference between the natural sciences and the *Geisteswissenschaften* has found its classic interpretation in the works of Heinrich Rickert, a philosopher of the Baden School.[10] Faithful to his Kantian views, Rickert based the distinction on a difference in method. True, he conceded in later years that a method is dependent on its object, but even so he maintained "that one cannot arrive at a full understanding of the *logical* character of the method of history until one has made abstraction from the distinctions which arise between various objects because of their content" (author's translation).[11] There are two ways, Rickert said, to consider reality: the generalizing method of the natural sciences and the individualizing one of history. Reality is transformed into nature when we consider it with regard to the general; it becomes history when we consider that same reality with regard to the individual. But not anything individual is thus *eo ipso* turned into something historical, only that which positively or negatively bears on values.[12] Value judgments are meta-historical in themselves, but it is up to the historian to see persons, things, and so forth, in their relation to values. For Rickert, also, it was here that the close link between history and philosophy manifested itself. In order to avoid a fairly widespread error about Rickert's views it seems useful at this moment to stress that he did not deny the individual aspect in the natural sciences and that he emphatically asserted that individuality in history could be the individuality of the whole, the historian being entitled to use general concepts. The important thing to Rickert, however, was that there is no univocal method in science, the characteristic difference being the one between the generalizing method of the natural sciences and the individualizing one of history, which for him was the representative of the human studies.[13]

Of course these few lines do not pretend to deal adequately with Rickert's doctrine. But it may be that the essential points of this "classic" theory will sufficiently indicate how right Gusdorf was when he suggested that the philosophy of the human studies was very slow in developing.[14] Unquestionably, Rickert's great merit is to have vindicated the claims of the human studies so that they have gained general recognition, in spite of the strong worldwide opposition of positivism, especially in Marxist and Anglo-Saxon countries. Nevertheless, the question of whether Rickert's solution points in the right direction is justified. Does some branch of knowledge change with a different method, or should we say, vice versa, that the method is changed because of a different discipline? A method, after all, does not make itself; as a way toward the truth it is found by focusing our attention on some special field of investigation, which on account of being this particular field is approached in a special way. Otherwise we would simply bypass the aim of the investigation, getting to know a particular area. In other words, here too we ought to apply the principle of intentionality: the act is specified by its object, the method is changed owing to a different discipline, the discipline is changed by a different object. Faithful to our starting point, the praxis of historical studies, we shall now attempt to define the object of this discipline. At the same time we may expect to see to what extent Rickert's distinction (subtle enough in itself) as regards method, individualizing or generalizing, should remain valid for the object of the science of history and hence for its method.

The object of historical science

"Popular" accounts of Rickert's theories are apt to state that for Rickert the object of history consists in things individual. In fact, such a pronouncement is unfair to the German philosopher, who has gone to great lengths to find a correct formula for the specific character of this object, emphasizing that things individual should always be seen in a general perspective, as part of the whole.[15] But his prudent example is by no means followed by every historian or philosopher. Jacques Maritain, for instance, states in *On the Philosophy of History*:

> History deals only with the singular and the concrete, with the contingent, whereas science deals with the universal and the necessary. History cannot afford us any explanation by universal *raisons d'être*. . . . its object as such is individual and singular. The explanation given by an historian, as historian, is an explanation of the individual, by the individual—by individual circumstances, motivations or events.[16]

As a matter of fact, it has become almost a commonplace to say that the object of history is the study of things individual. Yet it may be useful to measure this presumed "axiom" with the reliable yardstick of a phenomenological analysis of actual historical practice.

An analysis of man's self-realization in the past, of his growth in adultness does not leave the slightest doubt about the overriding importance of individual acts, facts, and dates for the praxis of history. We are concerned with self-realization here in time, implying an infinite succession of a variety of acts, events, and so forth. This variety makes it unavoidable that the study of history has to do with numerous other disciplines, ancillary and auxiliary ones, whose main concern is with individual facts in history. In order to be a good historian, a scholar should be sufficiently well versed in theology, philosophy, sociology, economics, philology, bibliography, archeology, and paleontology—all of which may be classified among the *ancillary sciences.*[17] "A man writing good history is driving more horses abreast in his theme than a man writing any other kind of literary matter."[18] Moreover, the study of history comprises another large group of so-called auxiliary sciences, which furnish the historian with his material and thus enable him to pursue his studies.

For the convenience of the layman in historical method, here are some brief definitions of these auxiliary sciences: *Chronology*, "the science of computing time," deals among other things with matters regarding the calendar. *Historical geography*, the corresponding discipline for space, has *onomastics* as one of its branches, at least for place names. *Genealogy* is "the study of family pedigrees." Next we have those branches of learning that bring us into contact with the sources of history themselves. The study of sources in general precedes *paleography*, "the study of ancient writing and writings as far as the seventeenth century." The *study of the incunabula and post-incunabula* teaches us about the oldest printed books. *Graphology* tries to infer character from handwriting. *Epigraphy* is "the knowledge of inscriptions." *Diplomatics*—that is, "the study of documents" in which the Benedictine Dom Mabillon was a pioneer—is in its turn assisted by *sphragistics* or "the study of seals." *Heraldry* is closely allied with genealogy. Further we have *numismatics*, "the study of coins"; *metrology*, occupying itself with weight and measures; and *statistics* (which, of course, serves other sciences as well), "the science dealing with the collection, analysis, interpretation, and presentation of numerical data."[19]

The mere list of all these ancillary and auxiliary sciences must inspire the layman with awe for the science of history and its devotees. But for the historian himself these numerous aids entail a great risk: the more help he gets, the more he may come to depend on it. In this way the splendid results of the increasingly perfected assistant sciences threaten to deflect the historian from his real task and drown him in overspecialization, so that his view of the object proper of history is obstructed. It was because of such a danger that Romein staked out the new ground of theoretical history, as we saw in Chapter I. But already in the early years of this century Trevelyan had sounded a warning.

> The danger to new countries with a population rapidly increasing is lest life there grow up rapidly into a raw materialism, a dead level of uniform ambition all directed to the mere acquisition of dollars. In the historical world the analogue of the almighty dollar is the crude document. If a student digs up a new document, he is happy, he has succeeded; if not, he is unhappy, he has failed.[20]

Materialism, surely, is not the most appropriate term for this ardent zeal, but fundamentally Trevelyan is right. It is the task of the auxiliary sciences to be of assistance to history, but all the separate facts and finds are in danger of becoming meaningless; history will be drowned in zealous overspecialization unless it is subordinated to its true aim, the improvement of our knowledge about the past of man. It is not the individual facts as such which are important but their place within the whole scheme. Facts constitute the material for the spirit of the historian, who gives them shape, makes them speak, and tells his

98

story with their help. By his inquiry, as I stated in Chapter II, the historian is faced with a chaos of facts; it is only through his methodological scrutiny that he will discover order and unity in this apparent chaos. In other words, history as a science cannot exist unless by the grace of a selection. It will never be possible for the historian to present us with a photographic picture of the past because he himself is always living in the present, and the past and the present cannot be made to coincide, to synchronize; life always goes on, time always continues. The historian merely turns to the past to ask a question of it; in the response elicited, the past reveals a pattern that previously was hidden to him. Individual facts are subordinated to this pattern. They have a function in the general scheme of things—by way of their importance for our knowledge of man in some particular period or country, for example. The object of historical research is not the individual fact but a totality of facts, insofar as they bear on man.

Thus we may say, provisionally, that the object of history is *man*. Contrary to what the expositions by Maritain and numerous others would seem to suggest, this does not stand for individual man. A story about some individual, a single human being, without a background, without being essentially directed toward other men and women around him, is not history in its true sense. Hemingway's *The Old Man and the Sea* is a brilliant story, but no one will call it history. This is not only because it belongs to the realm of fiction but also because it is timeless, elevated beyond the realm of time and space; it has no link with the factual happenings of history. Real history requires the aspect of man's concrete self-realization at some particular time and in some particular place. True, history can be the story of a single human being, but always in his relation to others; so it is at the same time a story about mankind. The individual man may be part of the object of history but only as related to his fellowmen. Marrou calls this the "Rule of the Epilogue."[21]

Any historical study that is not concerned with the story of mankind must begin with an introduction dealing with the antecedents of the matter in hand and must end with an epilogue. The fact is that real history is different from a novel, a play, a film. Of these *genres* of art a film's abrupt beginning and ending perhaps come closest to expressing the contrast with the science of history, for it is not possible to write history in this way. "Such is the unity of history that anyone who endeavors to tell a piece of it must feel that his first sentence tears a seamless web," according to the English historian Maitland.[22]

Therefore we now had better supplement our first, provisional formulation of the object of historical studies: the object of history is indeed man but is man in his relation to a people, to a civilization, to a human background, to his fellowmen. D'Arcy arrives at the same conclusion: "The examples . . . show that it is not so much the particular as the particular related to some pattern or intelligible whole."[23] In his subsequent description of the object he proposes to call the object of history "the quasi-particular"[24] rather than the particular or the general; his terminology does not seem to me to be very felicitous, but his views on the matter are quite right. His argument is a vindication of the phenomenon which the historian comes up against. But I would agree with the historian Huizinga rather than with the philosopher D'Arcy; Huizinga says:

> The historically general always remains particular because it has occurred only once. . . . The historically particular, on the other hand, derives its importance only from its pace *within* the general. . . . The object [of history] in general continues to be the actions and vicissitudes of people in community. [Author's translation.][25]

As a matter of fact, in history we have to do with man; that is, mankind in its numerous and diversified individuals, the general species, and the particular specimens. In technical terms it might be expressed another way. The object of historical science is the individual as related to the universal or, approached from the other side, the "historically universal," the *universale historicum*. The difference between this and the *universale physicum*, the "physically universal," is that the latter only points to an abstract mathematical universality and is not concerned as such with the realizations of the universal, insofar as mathematics is not concerned with reality as such. The *universale metaphysicum*, the "metaphysically universal," differs in that it deals with being as being, thus transcending time and space, whereas the "historically universal" implies a sequence in time and space. What is fundamental in history is the universality of the spirit, insofar as it is present in the successive individual appearances—the universal distributed over, and being present in, its individual representatives.

We would be far afield if we tried to find all this in the neo-Kantian Rickert; all the same I think we are justified in aligning his generalizing method with the *universale physicum* and its mathematical repeatability, considering his individualizing method parallel to the *universale historicum*, the general in the individual persons. Because of his Kantian attitude he tends to speak about method rather than about the object as norm, but doubtless his philosophy originated in close contact with the science of history. That is why we must not exaggerate the contrast. Some natural scientists—for example, biologists, astronomers, meteorologists—would not care simply to be associated with the generalizing method or the *universale physicum* because their science is concerned with life as such or deals with such individual events as a solar eclipse, some particular date, or tomorrow's weather. This is another sign that between natural and human sciences there is a distinction but not complete separation. For this reason, too, I believe that a historian would not recognize the object of his science if this were to be the individual, seeing that the individual fact is being subordinated to man and individual man to mankind in its growth toward maturity or the universal *in* the individual, in the technical terms used above—not in a metaphysical unity but in historical succession, the same humanity in the numerous, ever-varying appearances of man.

So may we define history as that branch of learning which aims at a systematic pursuit and handing down of knowledge about mankind's growth in adultness, insofar as this growth is revealed in the past.

The object of this science turns out to be man in his growth toward adulthood, insofar as this growth manifests itself in time and space, in the past.

A single point, finally, might demand elucidation. The addition of the words "in the past" could seem strange and appear to have been written down without reason, for not all philosophers of history are convinced that history deals with the past. Some scholars also wish to make the present and the future part of the study of history. I think there is little sense in going into this now. At our starting point, the praxis of historical studies, we met the historian bent over the human happenings of the past. That past, as we have found, is indissolubly linked with the present and the future, thus accounting for the making of history and enabling us to reflect on it. In this way the object of history does not exclude the present and the future. The historian speaks from the present; our thoughts on the future come within his province. These three dimensions are essential to history as a science, as they are to history as a happening. But in our reflection, and hence in our science, we have primarily and immediately to do with the past; hence the latter ought to have a place in the definition of the object of historical studies.

So far for the object in general. A further specification of this object is possible and essential with reference to the various divisions of history, according to how spiritual are its aspects. On the material level the quantitative moment and the physically universal will prevail; in the spiritual sphere the aspect of the unique will predominate. To economic history statistics will be most useful, but they will be less so for the history of philosophy. On the other hand, even the historian of philosophy cannot do without exact dates, and the student of economic history must not forget that his primary concern ought to be with man, not exclusively with a process of production relations running its inevitable course.

Self-knowledge

The fact, however, that the issue at stake is man (the spirit in its manifestations of increasing maturity), that the object is man in his phenomenal universality, implies that historical knowledge is necessarily self-knowledge. Man knows himself in his self-realization, while the spirit reflects upon itself in its manifestations.

If this is true, and it will be confirmed by our phenomenological analysis of historical praxis, the question again arises of how history can be a science. As a result of the active part of the historian, historical knowledge will always be subjective and, hence, one would be tempted to say, always lacking in objectivity. In other words: if history aims at being a science, its knowledge must needs be objective. But then, can there be any objectivity if an a priori is essentially and by its nature implied in its activity and cannot be removed from it? To this question historians and students of the philosophy of history give widely diverging answers. Before offering my own solution, I shall present two characteristic answers to this difficulty.

(1) The first answer to the question whether history can be a science if its cognitive method is closely bound up with subjectivity is proffered by those who try to eliminate all traces of the personal and the a priori. Equating history with positive science, they wish to apply the same method in both spheres. As supporters of this opinion could be mentioned the English historians J. Bury and T. Buckle, to whom I referred earlier. They are no more than representatives of the trend of positivism,

though, in the study of history, which may call the Frenchman H. Taine its most famous adherent.[26] Apart from the question whether it would be possible or essential to guard the positive sciences against any influence by the person of the scientist, the curious thing about the positivistic thesis is that while objecting to an a priori influence in history it seems to overlook the application of an a priori proper to a single method, the scientific one, in all branches of knowledge. Its advocates recognize only one method for all branches of knowledge; that is, the method used in the natural sciences. In this way they no longer have eyes for the analogy of the various disciplines, for the differences between the objects of the natural sciences and of history. In their zeal to defend objectivity these historians are apt to overlook the object.

According to them, objectivity is identical with general validity, any vital role by the practicing subject being ruled out. But as our phenomenological analysis of the praxis of historical studies has shown, this discipline is based on the cooperation between the question of the historian and its response by history as a happening. Both subject and object have to play their parts, and a selection from the chaotic whole by the subject, the historian, has always and necessarily been presupposed.

(2) Nowadays most historians will, in fact, be convinced of this, but all the same not an inconsiderable number of them continue to be tempted by the idea of general validity and the exactness of positive science. Doubtless the great German historiographer Leopold von Ranke was also familiar with this temptation, but the appeal to his famous phrase *wie es eigentlich gewesen* ("what actually happened") is often made in an unscholarly and unhistorical way, its context being ignored or omitted. Von Ranke did not aspire at all to be a scientist in historical matters; in making his statement he did not wish to give more than a modest, personal view of the historian's task: "To history has been assigned the office of judging the past, of in-

structing the present for the benefit of future ages. To such high offices this work does not aspire: It wants only to show what actually happened" (author's translation).[27] In other words, Von Ranke wants history to be itself, nothing more. He can hardly be styled a prophet of the scientific method in historical studies. This is shown by his works but also by his theoretical reflections about his own praxis. In the *Weltgeschichte* he testified:

> Nevertheless those historians are also mistaken who consider history simply an immense aggregate of particular facts which it behooves one to commit to memory; this results in the practice of heaping detail upon detail, held together only by some general moral principle. I believe rather that the discipline of history, at its highest, is called upon and has it in it to elevate itself in its own fashion from the investigation and observation of details to a universal view of events, to a knowledge of the objectively existing interrelationship. [Author's translation.][28]

How deep, however, this ideal of general validity can be rooted may be seen from Rickert, the great advocate of the specific nature of the human studies himself. If history is to be a science in its own right, he argues, it must be able to point to its general validity. According to the neo-Kantian philosopher, this is to be found in the general validity of values, a thing independent of the historian's personality; and it is for this reason that the scientific nature of history, in spite of its individualizing method, is being maintained.[29]

All supporters of this second opinion concede that it is extremely difficult, if not impossible, to safeguard oneself against all subjective influences, but in their discussions they turn out to be in favor of a maximum of objectivity and a minimum of subjectivity. They are out to minimize the a priori in an attempt to be as objective as possible; that is, objective and exact as in the positive sciences. When some years ago the Royal Dutch Academy of Sciences was celebrating its hundred-and-fiftieth anniversary, the historian Rogier, reviewing in his official speech

Huizinga's reflections on the specific nature of the human studies, said in his bold, unambiguous way:

> That the human studies cannot be subjected offhand to a mechanical investigation he considered their mark of nobility; I am inclined to think it an inconvenience. I would even venture further to call it a regrettable shortcoming of the human studies that they have not a sufficiently exact apparatus at their disposal. Of course I have reconciled myself to this—what else can I do? . . . Huizinga, I am afraid, would have thought it treason if a historian (as I venture to now) confessed to occasional twinges of jealousy toward science on account of its application of criteria that make timely discovery of error possible. There are moments when I yearn for some method which would eliminate all elements of subjectivity. [Author's translation.] [30]

From the wording of Rogier's feelings it will be clear, I believe, that theoretically there is something in the historian's nostalgia for the method of the natural sciences which does not quite fit. Scholars are convinced that they will never, of course, get to this paradise. Human studies should not wish to be as much as possible something else, only to be completely themselves. If in their method man has to play a part, it is no doubt a good thing to see to it that this aspect is not exaggerated, but it will be as important not to belittle it. Both extremes would derogate from scholarly praxis at this level—not only theoretically but, if the theory or philosophy is applied in its logical consequence (which, fortunately, is not always the case), also in actual practice. Thus one of its practical consequences might be that, when the subjective aspect is minimized, the true historian would not allow his normal human opinions, his national feelings, presumably his faith (when dealing with ecclesiastical history), to have a voice in the matter of his historical research, in order to remain objective at any price. Although those adhering to this view will be sure to add the qualifying phrase "as much as possible," it still remains to be seen whether such an attitude will serve the cause of historical studies, their philosophy and praxis. But I would like to go beyond this question for the moment. One thing, however, already seems clear: the advocates of the trend to minimize are manifestly led by a subjective dislike, partly explained as a reaction against the opinion to follow.

(3) The study of history may, indeed, be pursued in a way diametrically opposed to the two ways presented above. The influence of the personal, of the a priori, will be so strongly stressed that the actual facts (occasionally their factualness) may then be overlooked. This is especially the case with historical expositions presented by philosophers or theologians. An explicitly pragmatic history can be classified under this heading, generally speaking, because it will need special facts for a special purpose. Of course, minor variations of this idea abound. As its principal supporters may be singled out men like Augustine, Bossuet, Hegel, and Marx, but not all adherents are of such eminence; extremists do not hesitate to distort the facts for the benefit of their a priori concept. This is what Nazi historians did, and it will be remembered how after Stalin's death some years ago historians in the Soviet countries had to adjust their books. No less unscientific were those theological historians who managed to explain to us the exact supernatural significance of all kinds of particular events, evidently overlooking the essential truth of their faith that faith is a mystery, confided to human reason but always to be respected in its inscrutability. Though their exaggerations have been attributed to misguided piety, I wonder whether their attitude is not more proof of a rationalism pretending to be well informed about God's intentions than of veritable Christian faith.[31] On the other hand, the reaction of those who attempt to eliminate all influence of faith, even in Church history, may be making the same mistake when they set apart exclusively for the use of reason a sphere that transcends human reason as such.

(4) It would be incorrect, unfair even, to classify Romein with this third category, the stream of those who wish to place

very strong emphasis upon the influence of the subjective, even to the detriment of factualness. Although Romein openly acknowledges the influence of an a priori in one's view of history, and of his own Marxist a priori, he concedes at the same time that the crucial problem of theoretical history is the problem of objectivity. To quote once more his paradox, "A historian's value lies primarily in what he knows about man, rather than what he knows about the past."[32] Elsewhere he writes:

> It is obvious that the historian cannot possibly free himself of his own personality. He is—and remains—subject to a threefold subjectivity: of his *time*, of his *group* or class, of his *person*. The last is perhaps the easiest to overcome, the second more difficult, the first impossible. This has to do with the fact that it is impossible for us to size up our own times, hard to assess the group to which we belong, and in fact, relatively the easiest thing to see through ourselves. [Author's translation. Italics in original.][33]

The Dutch professor is fairly optimistic, I think, about our capacities for self-knowledge and perhaps somewhat pessimistic about our sensitivity to the spirit of our age. As we saw in Chapter I, because of an excessive commitment to history he has not succeeded in getting rid of all traces of relativism, but all the same his observations on the ways of historic thinking are particularly helpful. The most important thing for the historian, according to Romein, is the honest recognition that he himself is indeed a factor in his studies; being aware of this fact will help him to do his work with an essentially open mind.

> And who is going to attain such impartiality first and best? He, I daresay, who has an inner conviction about his point of view. He need not fear to weaken his own opinion by putting himself in another's position in order to do justice to it. [Author's translation.][34]

To do justice to the truth—such is also the purpose of the present work. Accordingly, I will try, having presented in detail the various and contrary opinions about the objectivity of historical thought, to state my own views. In doing so, my starting point will be still the same as that at the beginning of this book: the praxis of historical studies. Our phenomenological analysis of a historical investigation into the practice of philosophical-theological instruction over the first fifty years of the Dominican order demonstrated that history as a science owes its origin to the questioning historian, who by his questions creates a responsive unity. This unity is history as a happening, man in his growth in adultness, man in his self-realization. This implies, however, that history, which is the knowledge of man by man, can only exist by the grace of the cooperation between subject and object, both of which aspects are equally essential. Stressing the part of subject, we may say that history is self-knowledge; at the same time, history also knows about the other, which thereby excludes any arbitrariness on the part of the scholar. The questioning historian has to listen to the response of the past. History as a science will result from the dialogue between the working historian and the part of the past that he wishes to investigate, in the same way as history as a happening thrives on the encounter between man and his fellowman, between man and God.

For this reason the right way of putting questions and the right attitude when listening are of fundamental importance in historical research. All historical knowledge is based on some selection made by the historian. The past does not allow itself to be "photographed," assuming for the sake of our argument that a photograph is the ideal of "objective" reality and not the fine result of the photographer's work or even a clever fake. Anyhow, historical knowledge is never exhaustive. In Marrou's warning to those taking up historic studies, their guiding principle ought to be "not to think you are God almighty himself; do not forget you are only human" (author's translation).[35]

The truth unearthed by the historian is a human truth and therefore a partial one. I know the past but only insofar as I am capable of knowing it.[36] Or, to borrow another metaphor from Marrou, the historian is like a fisherman, who finds it impossible to catch all the fish of the past in his net.[37] This is unreservedly true for the historian as such. What fish he is going to catch, and how many, will essentially depend on his personality in the threefold, subjective sense of which Romein speaks. But this does not at all stand for untruth, for falsification. To make things clear Litt takes as an example the Battle of Leipzig in 1813. To Napoleon the sense of this battle was a different one before, during, and after the event. Similarly, our view of this feat of arms differs from what people thought about it in 1813, just as in the year 1813 there ran widely varying versions of it among the French, the English, the Germans, and the Dutch. All this variance concerns the same historical fact, the Battle of Leipzig.[38] These diverging views are not untrue because they diverge. On the contrary, in order to be true they have to be divergent. But then, any human knowledge is merely partial.

Geyl, who has some difficulty in stomaching Romein's honest admission that his own a priori provided him with certainty in his historical studies, on his part concedes as honestly that the multifarious and even contrary opinions of French historians about Napoleon are indispensable for our ever-improving view of the French emperor. According to him history is "a discussion without end . . . not leading to any generally accepted conclusion."[39] It will lead "to a gradual, if partial, conquest of reality,"[40] however. Geyl is too eminent a historian not to know from personal experience that the subjective plays an important part in historical research and that in this way we attain a knowledge of reality all the same; but he steers shy of Romein's resolute, logical thought and calls himself an adherent of historicism,[41] as Romein is a partisan of Marxism. Here we have another obvious example that the mere praxis of historical studies, and even the more penetrating theoretical history, is inadequate. We cannot devote ourselves to the study of history

110

without a philosophy of history. Now, this philosophy has discovered amidst a variety of opinions at least one point which
the majority of contemporary historians have in common: they
are agreed that in the discipline of history the subjective is to
play a part. It is essential for our argument to go into some detail here, and to consider what provisos have to be met from the
side of the scholar in order to attain the historian's ideal.

In the first place the historian has to be an integral human
being and in his case by implication an accomplished historian,
someone who has mastered the technique of his particular discipline, but in this sphere mere brains and technique are not
sufficient. A one-sided intellect coupled with the ever-perfected
techniques will saddle us with those dummies of the archives
mentioned by Ortega y Gasset[42] rather than produce real historians. If the historian is to attain his object—that is, man—he
will have to be open to this object, the quality of receptivity
presupposing a wealth of feelings, emotions, and imagination.
Eric Dardel, an expert historian himself, in his excellent little
book *L'Histoire, science du concret* (History, the Science of the
Concrete), stresses the fact that a historian who shuts himself
off from every feeling of generosity or pity does not set an example of objectivity but is a failure in this very respect. A lack
of subjectivity makes reality poorer, even falsifies it.[43]

But there is another point to this; namely, that we must not
exaggerate the role of the investigator (I have already referred
to this when mentioning those who maximize the a priori). All
good things can be abused. Feelings and emotions not only can
reveal historical truth; they may also hide or distort it. This
will also depend on the historian's moral honesty; therefore his
theoretical and practical ethics are of prime importance. Renier
would seem to underestimate this factor when he says, "The
judge of the story is the historian's own conception of honesty,
and that of other historians."[44] This may be true for areas that
are not likely to be swamped by National-Socialist or Communist

111

interpretations of history, such as Britain, for example, but it turns out that in less isolated places there is greater diversity of opinion about historical honesty, which makes the question of a less relativistic norm hard to avoid. Doubtless the first norm in the discipline of history ought to be a scholarly and not an ethical one. But as the autonomy of historical studies is not absolute, its norm requires further justification. Mere history cannot tell us why National-Socialism or Communism are unacceptable to us and why a different *Weltanschauung* should be preferable. For this we need ethical norms. Application of these norms, however, will in turn ask for an absolute basis, to be found ultimately not in philosophy but in religion, a religion revealed to us by him who said, "I am the way, and the truth, and the life" (John 14:6). Thus both ethics and religion are part of that wealth of "feelings" the historian's mind ought to possess.

We are touching here on the difficult theme of the relationship between science and religion. The argument about this issue is not closed yet; nor will it ever be, like any fundamental philosophical-theological problem. I shall not go into this now but shall only explain a single detail which could be useful at this stage.

To mention the role of religion in historical studies lays one open to the objection that this is an unscientific attitude, forcing the truth as it were instead of seeking for it assiduously. True, for the faithful Christian this risk is not imaginary; among those who overstated the case of the a priori in the discipline of history I have listed Christians and non-Christians alike. Of course, a host of minor scholars were in this respect a good deal worse than Augustine or Bossuet, but the possibility of abuse must not be a reason for us to rule out the religious act—according to Max Scheler the core of man's feelings—in the historian.[45] It is an essential part of his equipment.

This does not imply agreement with the nonsense that a non-Christian would not make a good historian, less even that a

112

good Christian by that very fact will be a good student of history. Very properly Rogier observes, "The fact of whether one belongs to one category or the other must not, in my opinion, have any effect at all on one's methods of investigation" (author's translation).[46] Now my point is that among the conditions to be met by the scholar in order to attain human fullness, religion should take an essential place and for that reason ought to be mentioned here. A good theologian will make it clear that this religion may be either implicit or explicit, but anybody lacking in openness toward the phenomenon of religion is thereby debarred from an important aspect of historical reality.

Such openness toward religious things is only one aspect of the general openness required in historical investigation and already mentioned earlier. For, as I said, history is no mere self-knowledge but knowledge of the other as well; sympathy for the other is a necessary condition for our knowledge of him.[47] Scheler reminds us hate makes blind and love opens our eyes to unexpected qualities in the other. Sympathy enables us to enter into the heart and the world of another, to understand him; not until we have done so can we set about writing history. Love, however, leads us to the truth and not to an idealized fictitious being, just as friends take each other as they are with their good and their bad qualities. Sympathy is the best basis for a correct critical attitude.

Up to now we have been mainly concerned with the important role of the historian as the subject in historical knowledge, but we shall get the same result by starting from its object. The principle *actus specificatur ab obiecto* ("the act receives its specification from the object"), in its modern version of phenomenological intentionality, will come to our aid here.

Since the object of historical studies is man in his self-realization, the historian's subject—that is, that part of his personality directed toward the object—will have to be fully human, or he will not be able to attain the object in its fullness.

113

All human qualities must be present as fully and harmoniously as possible if the selfsame qualities are to be discovered in the object. This is the way to arrive at true objectivity in the study of history.

What, then, is objectivity? It is neither the general validity of the natural sciences nor, as assumed by R. Voggensperger, being free of any affective moment.[48] Objectivity is analogous, indicating nothing more than a quality of human knowledge whereby we know reality as it is. Now since reality is infinitely varied (analogous, to use a technical term), objectivity, corresponding to this variety, will likewise be analogous. A univocal generalized validity as the only concept of objectivity is ruled out by the analogy of being. The objectivity must be different for the various branches of learning.

Let me try to clarify this by giving an example of its application in a special case; a thorny one, for that matter. I have already referred to the view of some historians who prefer a minimum of subjectivity and for that reason seek to eliminate the influence of supernatural faith in historical investigation, as a handicap to so-called objective science. In accordance with the interpretation of the analogy of objectivity as presented above, we shall now have to take an analogous view of historical objectivity. It is different for the various kinds of history. This means that for a particular sphere of history those historians are right. I hold that supernatural faith as such has no part in profane history because it is not explicitly present in the latter's object. Economic, cultural, and political history have to do with economics, culture, and politics, not with religion as such; therefore they should be assessed according to their own system of values. Things are different, however, when we have to do with Church history. Here the object is the growth of the community of men into the community of Christ, the realization of Christ's mystical body, a supernatural reality. Now a supernatural object can only be fully reached by a subject having "supernatural

114

eyes"; otherwise the historian will remain in the dark about the essence of the Church of Christ.

I repeat that this does not at all mean that a non-Catholic historian would not be capable of writing an excellent Church history or that he could not have openness, sympathy, and implicit faith. Nor must the Catholic historian consider his religion a substitute for his research; no doctrinal rule obliges him to gloss over the faults of members of the Church, of popes and bishops. The Bible does not do so, and he should not either. But, deepened by a sound theology, his faith will help him to overcome a possible one-sidedness in his argument since he knows Adam's fault, which gave us Christ, to have been a happy one. He will not allow himself to be cast down by the dark pages in the history of the Church because his theology is based on the fact that Christ has conquered "the world" and that this victory is being continued in his Church. To him the history of the Church is identical neither with political history nor with the policy of popes and bishops. He wants to devote his attention to the entire mystical body of Christ, all its members; to the lives of saints, whether they were public figures or led a hidden life; to the world of laymen, of priests, of the religious. Thus he is not a good Church historian if, for instance, in dealing with the nineteenth century in France he fails to mention the amazing spiritual work achieved in the confessional at Ars; the renewal of Catholic spirituality by a young Carmelite nun, Thérèse of Lisieux; the apparitions of our Lady at La Salette and Lourdes; the social work done by Albert de Mun; the charitable activities by Frédéric Ozanam, a layman; the liturgical renovations by Benedictine Dom Guéranger; the expansion of the missions; the doctoral thesis of a young Catholic philosopher, Maurice Blondel, and so on. I am aware of having omitted numerous important events, but the "positive" facts listed here, whose worldwide effects are still being felt, are adequate, I think, for my present purpose; namely, to give the reader an idea of what

115

elements are essential for the object of Church history. Incidentally, I would like to see included among them the workings of the Holy Ghost outside the directly visible Church.

If the object of Church history is understood in this way, our conclusion is bound to be that Church history belongs to the realm of theology, is a theological discipline, and presupposes faith and theology in its subject, the Church historian.

Having applied, as a practical example, our views regarding the attainment of historical knowledge to the department of theology, let us now return to philosophy and conclude this section with a quotation from Edmund Husserl. Toward the end of his life this pioneer of phenomenology became fascinated by the phenomenon of history. A manuscript dating from 1936, which deals with the method of historical studies, has been left us by chance, although its self-critical author headed it by the marginal note: "Unripe material, Part I. In fact not worth the paper it is written on; fit only for the wastepaper basket" (author's translation). What struck me at the very beginning of this fragment was Husserl's remark that all reflection is preceded by a naïve attitude which first indulges in action until the experience of failure brings it to a standstill and hence toward reflection. This, as we have seen, has been exactly the course of historical studies in our day: the actual practice of history having run aground, scholars have been compelled to turn again to its theory and philosophy. In these philosophical activities Husserl, starting from the historian's experience, underlines the importance of the role the historian has to play in historical studies:

> Here we must keep in mind that the historian can never forget himself, that thematically he is part of that universal historical horizon which he is exploring. He himself as person is a member of the universal historical existence. His life in the present world is a moment of the universal historical life of mankind, which is his universal theme. However narrowly [replaced in the margin by *widely*] he may circumscribe his specific theme, thematically

116

he cannot entirely be released from it. *Any experience of mine, any limiting statement* about others made by me in my life, necessarily emanates from myself. To me, others are others from my own point of view; it is from my own experience that they exist for me and exist like that . . . I am always present at these scenes as the person I am . . . The kind of history that would be capable of establishing definitely [in the margin *temporally*] "how things actually happened," is in principle an impossibility. Aiming to orientate the historian's methodological ideal by a concept of truth that is in principle [in the margin *essentially*] the same as in the natural sciences—this would mean setting out upon a wild-goose chase. [Author's translation. Italics in original.][49]

Knowledge at a distance

One special difficulty of historical knowledge remains to be dealt with: the problem that in history our knowledge is always knowledge at a distance, the distance from the present to the past. In the natural sciences things as a rule are different. With them, unless the historical dimension of reality is explicitly coming up for discussion, I am able to verify the data because I have them in my hands; I can touch them, see, smell, or hear them—apprehend them tangibly somehow by means of the senses. But the verification of psychological data, of my judgment of others, is a much more delicate affair, based as it is on the testimony of the individual with whom I am dealing. Here the skillful use of some recognized psychological test may render valuable assistance. Police forces might resort to special investigation methods, the lie detector, or even truth drugs. We may question whether it will ever be possible to know a human being by means of such judicial procedures, but we have through them, at least, a chance to learn by direct contact something about some particular fact. In order to know a person in his individuality the police take his fingerprints; ordinary people in most countries can be identified by means of their passports or other identification.

117

In the study of history the role of the passport is taken over by documents, written evidence or other material. The historian has to use them as a substitute for direct contact with the individual who is the object of his search. Occasionally he may think that he has come very close to him, for instance when he has been so fortunate as to discover that person's diary, although an experienced historian knows that even the data supplied by a diary have to be verified. Even a diary may deceive, willfully or unintentionally; anyhow, it presents a one-sided view that requires completion from other sources. Since man is a mystery, this cannot be otherwise; it is impossible to know him completely. So the historian continues to pile up more documents. But the difficulty remains that a mere piling up of documents will never bridge the gulf between the past and the present, will never close the gap. Yet some people think this is possible; they prefer a historical knowledge based on more documents to a less documented one. Thus the neo-Spinozist Henri Sérouya admires both Christ and Spinoza, but his preference is for the latter because he is closer to us in history, because we have better and more recent documentation about him.[50] Such an attitude tends to see the essence of history in the piling up of documents. Young nations especially are prone to this temptation. American historians can utilize such a mass of data about the brief history of their own nation that they are in danger of becoming no more than gatherers of minute facts.

> A side effect of this specialty is that encyclopedic fullness of detail has tended to absorb the energies of our historians; they hesitate to advance broad syntheses, preferring to establish masses of related facts rather than to venture views on their philosophic significance. No fact seems too small to deserve recording, even in works for the general public.[51]

It is the danger of overspecialization, which I mentioned in Chapter I when stressing the need for theoretical history and for a philosophy of history. We may ask again whether this fashion of document hunting is the right one to bridge the gap between the past and the present.

Even accepting the necessity for documentation, our answer must be No. The first reason is that overspecialization does not advance the cause of history but drowns it in its materials. A more intrinsic argument is that when historians are complaining about the difficulty of knowing the past because it is so remote from the present in which they live, we have to deny the assumption, for the past is not remote. Who says so has fallen victim to a manner of "tangible thinking," which touches everything at a certain level but human reality. In fact, we have seen that we ourselves are the past. Man is that amazing triunity of past, present, and future because he is a historical being. There is no need for him to seek after history, to grope in the dark; history is just the expression of his own being. The past is always present in me, and I can grasp it, by means of my memory, that living bond between the present and the past. My memory enables me to reflect upon the past, and the "extension" of this memory is what constitutes the study of history. Thus historical science finds its ontological basis in my historical existence. Temporal distance (of which, of course, I am always aware) is compensated for by the fact that the past on which I am reflecting is always my own past, essentially one with my present and my future.

Moreover, the documentary method and all the other achievements of the auxiliary sciences, though absolutely essential, are not sufficient in themselves because they do not enable me to know the object of my historical studies; namely, man in the past. It stands to reason that one must verify the authenticity of one's material. We ought to be grateful that for this we have ever better means at our disposal. But do we arrive in this way at a real knowledge of the past? Do I really know Socrates when I know that some particular work by Plato is authentic? Or, to make matters less complicated, do I really know Plato from his

119

authentic works? We learn from a letter, considered authentic, by the Athenian philosopher that he deemed it impossible to represent his teaching in a written corpus. What, then, about our knowledge of his person? Even if this be true, if our documents turn out to fail in their task of giving us a true understanding of man in the past, what is there to direct the discipline of history toward its object?

Let us not worry greatly about this apparent impasse but return to the parallel from daily life which was just mentioned: do we really know the man who shows us his authentic passport? To be sure, we know that the passport is his and through it that he must be an American, British, Dutch, or some other foreign national. But do we, by knowing about him, know the man himself? Later, in the airplane, we may have a talk with him; he may show us snapshots of his wife, his children, his home, and in this way we may get to know more about him, perhaps even to know him. Through his words, his behavior under ordinary circumstances, maybe under unusual or difficult ones, by numerous signs interpreted by us, a superficial contact may grow into a real encounter with this individual. It is then that we truly have come to know him.

Such knowledge, however, is not the result of speculative, scientific thinking.

> Our knowledge of an individual's spiritual personality is not discursive: a consciousness is not to be constructed from the outside; one's inner personality cannot be reached as the final term of a series of abstract terms. The discursive function of our intellect can prepare the way for the apprehension of some concrete existence, but it cannot itself accomplish this act. It is unable to realize that phenomenon of overall interpretation which constitutes the discovery of some personality similar to mine; less even can it penetrate into the secret of that spiritual personality which is at the same time both unique and fraternal. Even supposing that the "spiritual core" of a human being could reveal itself to another, as Scheler would have it, this would still have to occur at

120

a nondiscursive level. Existence and value of the human personality elude this function of the intellect; they remain "obscure" to it. Besides, we have to admit that this perception is not the luminous penetration of an inner reality. Far more is it the all-encompassing approach to a spiritual existence, a kind of *contact* and *concurrence* with the discovered being—both of them allowing of limitless study, but in part opaque and resistant to reason. It is here that the act of faith is situated, and consequently it places itself on a plane that is obscure and exasperating to pure reason: the universe of persons is a world to which we can only gain real admittance through love. [Author's translation. Italics in original.] [52]

The French theologian Mouroux is speaking here about our knowledge of the human person in relation to personal cognition as it occurs in supernatural faith. But his argument leads to a more general conclusion: knowledge of an individual's personality demands belief, natural belief. Natural belief is to be taken as a function of human knowledge whereby the human intellect assents to truth, not because of the perspicuity of the object, but on account of its goodness. The assent is given not on account of truth as truth but on account of the truth to be found in the good. Thomism here speaks of *cognitio per connaturalitatem* ("cognition through affinity"). [53] Influenced by phenomenology and existentialism (the latter taken in a very wide sense, including Newman and Blondel as well as Heidegger and Sartre), we have been taught the importance of cognition by way of vital experience, a form of belief in which the influence of free will on human reason is honestly acknowledged. In fact, we can hardly do otherwise if we lend a faithful ear to the language of phenomena. Belief is an aspect of human knowledge at all levels, even in the natural sciences, but its function becomes manifest in the human studies, philosophy and theology. Owing to the influence of the human will in all human cognition, certainty is free. This is not an arbitrary judgment but, on the contrary, one based on respect for the phenomena.

Human beings that we are, we have to start our knowledge by an initial acceptance of reality, a reality consisting of ourselves together with the other spiritual and material beings around us in this world. In any judgment this aspect of acceptance, of freedom is contained. Such is what I could denote here belief, natural belief, which by its essence asks for further justification from our speculative reason. To prevent any misunderstanding, it seems important in this context to state that this kind of cognition is true knowledge, in which love plays a vital part, though not as a substitute for the intellect. Love as such cannot know. That is the function of the intellect, be it either practical or speculative. Because of this twofold aspect of human knowledge we are entitled to speak of human sciences (human studies) and of history as a science.

And thus we have come back to history, for the sake of which we so greatly digressed. We asked ourselves how, after all, it is possible for history to ascertain its object if documents cannot give us a real knowledge of man in the past. My answer that because this impasse was only an apparent one we were not to worry can now be clarified by applying the theory of connatural cognition. Documents and other aids are indispensable if we are to arrive at a knowledge of man in the past, but they only represent the discursive aspect of the historical method. In order to attain a real knowledge of our object we need something more than mere reasoning intellect. In the same way as in psychology and other human studies, so in history, too, we ought to stress the essential role of natural belief—or, in other words, of connatural cognition. That is the reason that I referred earlier to sympathy and love as necessary provisos in the person of the historian, enabling him to reach out to the past by way of affinity. He should utilize his documents as signs that point the way to man's deeper reality. They can help him grasp through his practical intellect that human reality of which they are the expression.

122

Of course, the historian may be handicapped by this dimension of the past. Herein the auxiliary sciences, which can help him to understand the strange and remote language that documents are apt to speak, will prove indispensable. Often it will only be after hard toil that he will find the hidden secret in research. It may be a slight comfort to him, however, to learn that knowledge about the present is still more difficult to obtain, if not impossible (the view of Hegel and Romein). His research and the interpretation of his material enable the historian to discern a unity in the welter of past occurrences, but how is he to apply these scientific methods to topical news? how to make a good selection from the tangle of facts? how to find his way through the maze of daily events? how to discover what is important and what not?—unless it be by waiting patiently. Time will be the first to answer these questions for him by making a provisional selection. Then the historian can set to work.

Hence the student of history has not many misgivings about knowing things from a distance. That very distance is essential if he is to arrive at the kind of knowledge that meets scholarly standards. The philosopher of history can help to explain this fact by his discovery that, properly speaking, the problem of knowing things from a distance is a fictitious one because man himself is the past he is investigating. Speculative knowledge and practical knowledge merge into the discipline of history.

*   *   *

This brings me to the end of my argument. All along I have tried to remain faithful to my original starting point of the philosophy of history—that is, the science of history—and not to lose contact with it. A phenomenological analysis of historical praxis revealed the main divisions of history—divisions found again in this book—history as a happening and history as a science. In order to assert the latter's claims as a separate branch of learning it was necessary to determine its object and to elucidate the nature of its knowledge. In this way the complex character of history gradually evolved. It always deals with man. Man, however, can be considered at many levels of his complex being. Church history and secular history, the latter supplying us with as many subdivisions as there are values in human life, thus distinguish themselves.

As a philosopher I can speak about the meaning of history as such, but I am not qualified to argue about particular points either of Church history or of profane history and its numerous branches. Neither the historian nor the philosopher is qualified to determine the significance of, for example, American or British history. A competent historian, no doubt, would be able to tell us something about the importance of the American people in the past, but his knowledge of the present and the future is inadequate, and therefore on the whole he can only guess about that period. Indeed, by revelation the theologian may know a good deal about the significance of such a special nation as the Jews, but even in that realm he can do no more than speculate about the nature of the link between its contemporary profane history and its final destination.

Nevertheless, the certainty of the philosophy of history is not upset by its limitations and by the fact that it has to restrict itself to the province of philosophy, to history as a happening. The idea that history is not something senseless but that in it man progresses toward self-realization—and that it depends on the free cooperation of individuals, whether this will be to the good or to the bad—may be a powerful stimulant for the history we are making together today.

NOTES

CHAPTER I

1 Johan Huizinga, "Mijn weg tot de historie," *Verzamelde werken* (Haarlem: H. D. Tjeenk Willink en Zoon, 1948-1953), I, 36.

2 Huizinga, "Cultuurhistorische verkenningen," *Verzamelde werken*, VII, 35-94; translated in *Men and Ideas* (New York: Meridian Books, 1959), pp. 17-76. Huizinga, "De wetenschap der geschiedenis," *Verzamelde werken*, VII, 134-50; translated in Fritz Stern, editor, *The Varieties of History: From Voltaire to the Present* (New York: Meridian Books, 1956), pp. 289-303.

3 José Ortega y Gasset, *Obras Completas*, Vol. IV: *La "Filosofía de la Historia" de Hegel y la Historiología* (Madrid: Revista de Occidente, 1957), pp. 521-41. See also J. H. Nota, S.J., "Le Point de départ de la philosophie de l'histoire," in *Proceedings of the Eleventh International Congress of Philosophy*, Brussels, August 20-26, 1953 (14 vols. Amsterdam: North-Holland Publishing Company; Louvain: Editions E. Nauwelaerts, 1953), VIII, 10 ff.

4 Jan Romein, "Theoretical History," *Journal of the History of Ideas*, 9 (1948), 53 ff.

5 G. J. Renier, *History: Its Purpose and Method* (Boston: Beacon Press, 1950), p. 78.

6 Ortega y Gasset, *Obras Completas*, IV, 537.

7 Marc Bloch, *Apologie pour l'histoire ou métier d'historien* (Paris: Colin, 1949), p. xvii; translated as *The Historian's Craft*, from the French by Peter Putnam (Manchester: Manchester University Press, 1954).

8 Romein, *In de hof der historie* (Amsterdam: Querido, 1951), pp. 9-53.

9 Romein, *Journal of the History of Ideas*, 9 (1948), 58.

10 Fritz Wagner, *Geschichtswissenschaft* (Freiburg: Alber, 1951). See also *Moderne Geschichtsschreibung* (Berlin: Duncker und Humblot, 1960).

11 J. van der Pot, *De periodisering der geschiedenis*, met een voorwoord van J. Romein (The Hague: Van Stockum, 1951), pp. vii ff.

12 Romein, *Journal of the History of Ideas*, 9 (1948), 55 ff.

13 Romein, *In de hof der historie*, pp. 105 ff.

14 Romein, *Journal of the History of Ideas*, 9 (1948), 55.

15 R. Aron, *Introduction à la philosophie de l'histoire* (Paris: Gallimard, 1948).

CHAPTER II

1 Bloch, *Apologie pour l'histoire*, p. xiv.

2 Huizinga, *Verzamelde werken*, VII, 51, 154 ff.; translated in Huizinga, *Men and Ideas*, pp. 33 ff.

3 Stern, editor, *The Varieties of History*, p. 18.

4 E. Lousse, *Geschiedenis* (Bruges: De Kinkhoren, 1945), p. 18.

5 R. Voggensperger, *Der Begriff der Geschichte als Wissenschaft im Lichte aristotelisch-thomistischer Prinzipien* (Freiburg: Paulus-Verlag, 1948), p. 14.

6 "Human studies" was suggested as a translation of *Geisteswissenschaften* by Professor A. W. P. Wolters of Reading University to his colleague Herbert A. Hodges (*Wilhelm Dilthey: An Introduction* [London: Kegan Paul, Trench, Trubner and Company, 1944], p. 157).

7 Huizinga, *Verzamelde werken*, VII, 84.

8 F. van der Meer, *Geschiedenis van een kathedraal* (Utrecht: Spectrum, 1961).

9 See Henri I. Marrou, *De la Connaissance historique* (Paris: Editions du Seuil, 1954), pp. 60 ff.; translated as *The Meaning of History* (Baltimore: Helicon Press, 1966).

10 As quoted by Bloch, *Apologie pour l'histoire*, p. 90.

11 Charles H. Haskins, *The Renaissance of the Twelfth Century* (Cambridge: Harvard University Press, 1927), pp. 8 ff.

12 Pot, *De periodisering der geschiedenis.*

13 See Romein, *In de hof der historie*, pp. 55 ff.

14 Martin Heidegger, *Sein und Zeit* (Halle: Max Niemeyer, 1941), p. 376; translated by John Macquarrie and Edward Robinson as *Being and Time* (New York: Harper and Row, 1962).

15 Ibid., p. 375.

CHAPTER III

1 I have refrained from giving detailed references at this stage because they are to be found either in the bibliography or in the course of this work.

2 M. C. Smit, *De verhouding van Christendom en historie in de huidige rooms-katholieke geschiedbeschouwing* (Kampen: Kok, 1950), p. 15. Subsequent Dutch publications, such as those by Bellon and Delfgaauw, have not effected an essential change in the situation.

3 Voltaire used the term for the first time in 1756. It also appears in the preface to the *Essai sur les moeurs et l'esprit des nations* of 1765.

4 Karl Löwith, *Meaning in History: The Theological Implications of the Philosophy of History* (Chicago: University of Chicago Press, 1949).

5 Ibid., p. 198.

6 See M. C. D'Arcy, *The Meaning and Matter of History: A Christian View* (New York: Meridian Books, 1961), pp. 150 ff.

7 M. F. Sciacca, "Vi è una filosofia della storia?" in *Proceedings of the Tenth International Congress of Philosophy*, Amsterdam, August 11-18, 1948, edited by E. W. Beth and others (Amsterdam: North-Holland Publishing Company, 1949), Fasc. II, p. 990.

8 Marrou, "Philosophie critique de l'histoire et 'sens de l'histoire,'" in *L'Homme et l'histoire: Actes du sixième congrès des sociétés de philosophie en langue française* (Paris: Presses Universitaires de France, 1952), pp. 3 ff.

9 "Par définition et par essence, la métaphysique veut arracher au monde son dernier secret, son sens *absolu*, je veux dire le sens que le monde a pour Dieu lui-même . . ." (L. Malevez, "La Vision chrétienne de l'histoire," *Nouvelle Revue Théologique*, 71 [1949], 113 ff., 244 ff.).

10 "Mais le sens que l'homme ne lit pas dans le phénomène, le croyant l'affirme . . ." (ibid., p. 257). See also Emerich Coreth, *Grundfragen des menschlichen Daseins* (Innsbruck: Tyrolia Verlag, 1956), pp. 78 ff.

11 Karl Jaspers, *The Origin and Goal of History*, translated from the German by Michael Bullock (New Haven: Yale University Press, 1953), pp. 45-46.

12 Ibid., p. 46.

13 Ibid., p. 71.

14 T. Litt, *Wege und Irrwege geschichtlichen Denkens* (Munich: Piper and Company, 1948), p. 10.

15 Georg Wilhelm Friedrich Hegel, *Phänomenologie des Geistes* (Leipzig: Meiner, 1921), p. 196.

16 "Par *sens,* par *signification* de l'histoire, ils désignaient, un peu confusément, sa direction et plus encore sa valeur par rapport au fins dernières" (Malevez, "Deux Théologies catholiques de l'histoire," *Bijdragen der Nederlandse Jezuieten*, 10 [1949], 225).

17 Löwith, *Meaning in History*, p. 5. Compare with Romein, *Tussen vrees en vrijheid* (Amsterdam: Querido, 1950), p. 227. The French word *sens* signifies "sense" as well as "direction."

18 Jaspers, *The Origin and Goal of History*, p. 233.

19 Ibid., p. 264.

20 St. Irenaeus, *Adversus haereses*, 4:20, 1; P. G. 7, 1037.

21 Ibid.

22 ". . . l'hellénisme n'est jamais parvenu à élaborer une philosophie et moins encore, une théologie de l'histoire" (H. C. Puech, "La Gnose et le temps," in *Eranos-Jahrbuch*, 1951 [Zurich: Rhein-Verlag, 1952], p. 63).

23 B. A. van Groningen, *In the Grip of the Past: Essay on an Aspect of Greek Thought* ("Philosophia Antiqua," Vol. VI. Leiden: E. J. Brill, 1953), p. 42.

24 Herodotus, *Histories*, I, 207:2; translated by Aubrey de Selincourt (Baltimore: Penguin Books, 1954).

25 Thucydides, *The Peleponnesian War*, I, 22:4; translated by Rex Warner (London: Cassell and Company, 1962).

26 Polybius, *Histories*, VI:6; translated by W. R. Paton (6 vols. "Loeb Classical Library." Cambridge: Harvard University Press, 1954).

27 Homer, *Iliad*, VI, 146-49.

28 Mircea Eliade, *Cosmos and History: The Myth of the Eternal Return* (New York: Harper and Brothers, 1959), pp. 20 ff.

29 G. Gusdorf, *Mythe et métaphysique* (Paris: Flammarion, 1953), pp. 11 ff.

30 "Le mythe est senti et vécu avant d'être intelligé et formulé. Il est la parole, la figure, le geste, qui circonscrit l'événement au coeur de l'homme, émotif comme un enfant, avant que d'être récit fixé" (M. Leenhardt, "Do Kamo," *Nouvelle Revue Française*, 1947, p. 247 [as quoted by Gusdorf, *Mythe et métaphysique*, p. 16]).

31 Eliade, *Cosmos and History*, p. 26.

32 Gusdorf, *Mythe et métaphysique*, pp. 65 ff.

33 W. Nestle, *Vom Mythos zum Logos* (Stuttgart: Kröner, 1940).

34 G. Krüger, *Einsicht und Leidenschaft: Das Wesen des platonischen Denkens* (Frankfurt: Klostermann, 1948), p. 66.

35 Plato, *Phaedo*, 114d; translated in *Apology, Crito, Phaedo, Phaedrus* ("Loeb Classical Library." Cambridge: Harvard University Press, 1953), p. 391.

36 Werner Jaeger, *Aristotle* (second edition translated by Richard Robinson; New York: Oxford University Press, 1948), p. 378.

37 Aristotle, *Metaphysica*, A, 2, 982b, 18-19.

38 Van Groningen, *In the Grip of the Past*, pp. 1 ff.

39 Plato, *Timaeus*, 37d.

40 Lucretius, *De natura rerum*, III, 945; V, 1135.

41 Aristotle, *Problemata*, XVII, 3. See also Puech, in *Eranos-Jahrbuch*, 1951, pp. 60 ff. For Epicurus as an exception see p. 65, n. 10.

42 Siegfried Lauffer, "Der antike Fortschrittsgedanke," in *Proceedings of the Eleventh International Congress of Philosophy*, XII, 37 ff.

43 Plato, *Phaedo*, 67a; *Phaedrus*, 249c; *Republic*, 540b. An exception for "the bad" is the myth of Er, in the *Republic*, 614 ff.

44 Eliade, *Cosmos and History*, p. 48. For Mazdeism—history's end is that the bad receive their just reward but the good revert to their origin, retaining the circle—see H. Corbin, "Le Temps cyclique dans le Mazdéisme et dans l'Ismaélisme," in *Eranos-Jahrbuch*, 1951, pp. 149 ff. Zarathustra—Nietzsche notwithstanding—was the only sage not to teach the eternal cycle.

45 For a treatment of this problem in general see Oscar Cullmann, *Christ and Time: The Primitive Conception of Time and History*, translated from the

German by Floyd F. Filson (Revised edition. Philadelphia: Westminster Press, 1964).

46 Löwith, *Meaning in History*, p. 166.

47 ". . . viam rectam sequentes, quae nobis est Christus, eo duce ac salvatore a vano et inepto impiorum circuitu iter fidei mentemque avertamus" (St. Augustine, *De Civitate Dei*, XII, 20 [P. L. 41:370]).

48 "Haec tamen septima erit sabbatum nostrum, cujus finis non erit vespera, sed dominicus dies velut octavus aeternus, qui Christi resurrectione sacratus est, aeternam non solus spiritus, verum etiam corporis requiem praefigurans. Ibi vacabimus, et videbimus; videbimus et amabimus; amabimus et laudabimus. Ecce quod erit in fine sine fine" (ibid., XXII, 30 [P. L. 41:804]).

49 P. Ariès, *Le Temps de l'histoire* (Monaco: Du Rocher, 1954), p. 105. See also M. D. Chenu, "Conscience de l'histoire et théologie au douzième siècle," *Archives d'histoire doctrinale et littéraire du Moyen Age*, 21 (1954), 107 ff.

50 Joachim of Fiore, *Das Reich des heiligen Geistes*, bearbeitung Alfons Rosenberg (Munich: Barth, 1954).

51 "Et per hoc etiam excluditur quorumcumque vanitas qui dicerent esse expectandum aliud tempus Spiritus Sancti. . . . Ad quartum dicendum quod cum Christus statim in principio evangelicae praedicationis dixerit: "Appropinquavit regnum caelorum," stultissimum est dicere quod Evangelium Christi non sit Evangelium regni" (St. Thomas Aquinas, *Summa Theologica*, I-II, 106, 4, in c. et ad obj.). Compare with *Supplementum*, III, 77, 1, in c. et ad 4.

52 Löwith, *Meaning in History*, p. 104.

53 François Marie Arouet de Voltaire, "Introduction," *Essai sur les moeurs et l'esprit des nations*, in *Oeuvres complètes* (Paris: Renouard, 1819), XIII, 157.

54 Hegel, *Phänomenologie des Geistes*, p. 44. On Hegel's philosophy of history see William H. Dray, *Philosophy of History* (Englewood Cliffs: Prentice-Hall, 1964), pp. 67 ff.

55 Hegel, *Phänomenologie des Geistes*, p. 12.

56 Ibid., pp. 127 ff., and Encyclopädie der Philosophischen Wissenschaften (Leipzig: Meiner, 1920), pp. 376 ff. See also the critical exposition in G. Fessard, "Esquisse du mystère de la société et de l'histoire," *De l'Actualité historique* (Bruges: Desclée de Brouwer, 1960), I, 121 ff.

57 Hegel, *Philosophie der Weltgeschichte* (Leipzig: Meiner, 1920), pp. 39 ff.

58 Karl Marx and Friedrich Engels, "Manifesto of the Communist Party," in *Basic Writings on Politics and Philosophy*, edited by Lewis S. Feuer (Garden City: Doubleday and Company, 1959), p. 29.

59 Jaspers, *The Origin and Goal of History*, p. 251.

60 G. Wetter, *Der dialectische Materialismus* (Vienna: Herder, 1952), pp. 246 ff., 445 ff.

61 Friedrich Nietzsche, *Nachgelassene Werke* (Leipzig: Naumann, 1901), Bd. XII, n. 105, p. 57.

62 Simone de Beauvoir, *Tous les Hommes sont mortels* (Paris: Gallimard, 1946).

63 J. L. Ferrier, "La pensée anhistorique de Sartre," in *L'Homme et l'histoire*, pp. 171 ff.

64 "Je considère le marxisme comme l'indépassable philosophie de notre temps" (Jean-Paul Sartre, *Critique de la raison dialectique* [Paris: Gallimard, 1960], p. 9).

65 Ibid., p. 23.

66 Ibid., pp. 63, 754 ff.

67 Jaspers, *The Origin and Goal of History*, pp. 231 ff.

68 Ibid., p. 264. A résumé of Jaspers' views may be found in his *Einführung in die Philosophie* (Zurich: Artemis, 1950), pp. 92 ff. Heidegger has already been referred to.

69 Jaspers, *The Origin and Goal of History*, pp. 264 ff.

70 Ibid., p. 261. See also Jaspers, *Einführung in die Philosophie*, p. 101.

71 Jaspers, *Von der Wahrheit* (Munich: Piper and Company, 1948), pp. 832 ff.

72 Josef Pieper, *The End of Time: A Meditation on the Philosophy of History*, translated by Michael Bullock (New York: Pantheon Books, 1954), pp. 44 ff.

73 See pp. 24 ff. of this work.

74 Bloch, *Apologie pour l'histoire*, p. 107.

75 Löwith, *Meaning in History*, pp. 60 ff.

76 As quoted by Löwith in *Meaning in History*, p. 60.

77 Pieper, *The End of Time*, pp. 89 ff.

78 Johann G. Fichte, *Die Grundzüge des gegenwärtigen Zeitalters*, in *Sämmtliche Werke* (Berlin, 1846), VII, 18.

79 Löwith, *Meaning in History*, p. 60.

80 E. Rothacker, *Logik und Systematik der Geisteswissenschaften* (Bonn: Bouvier, 1948), pp. 80 ff.

81 "Im Ganzen aber steht das Menschengeschlecht, wie die Welt überhaupt, unter dem allgemeinen Gesetze der Entwicklung, vermöge dessen alles im Fortgange oder Fortschritte begriffen ist . . . Daher steht das Menschengeschlecht unstreitig jetzt auf einer höhern Bildungsstufe, als zu irgend einer frühern Zeit, sowohl extensiv als intensiv. Es hat Fortschritte gemacht, kann deren machen und soll es auch, da man zu keiner Zeit sagen kann, dass das Menschengeschlecht so sei, wie es nach den unabweisslichen Forderungen der Vernunft sein soll" (W. Krug, *Allgemeines Handwörterbuch der philosophischen Wissenschaften* [Leipzig, 1827], II, 54).

82 "Progress," Encyclopedia Americana, 1946, XXII, 634. A superior article on the subject has since appeared in the 1965 edition.

83 Ibid.

84 M. Langeveld, "Psychology and Physiology of Man," in *Verkenning en verdieping* (Purmerend: Muuses, 1950), p. 159.

85 Romein, *Het onvoltooid verleden* (Amsterdam: Querido, 1948), p. 39, n. 1.

86 Bernard Delfgaauw, *Geschiedenis en vooruitgang* (Baarn: Wereldvenster, 1961), I, 27 ff.

87 Romein, *Het onvoltooid verleden*, p. 94.

88 Reinhold Niebuhr, *Faith and History* (New York: Charles Scribner's Sons, 1949), pp. 7 ff.

89 Romein, *Het onvoltooid verleden*, pp. 13 ff., 30 ff. In his *Carillon der tijden* (Amsterdam: Querido, 1953), pp. 12 ff., Romein uses the term *voortgang* ("advancement") instead of *vooruitgang* ("progress").

90 Aristotle, *Metaphysica*, 7, 1072b, 26-27.

91 ". . . ni la morale, ni même le 'spirituel' dans le sens immanent où le mot
    est trop généralement entendu, ne pouvaient avoit le moindre effet sensible
    sur l'évolution de la société. Le monde de l'asservissement et de la destruc-
    tion de l'homme ne pouvait être contrebattu par une technique plus raffinée,
    plus subtile, mais rompu seulement par l'irruption, dans le monde visible,
    d'un monde invisible ayant ses racines dans le Transcendance: celui du
    Pauvre et du Mendiant éternel, de la sainteté eschatologique, celui du Dieu
    Vivant et de l'Eglise Vivante" (M. Moré, "Liminaire," *Dieu Vivant*, 16
    [1950], 11).

92 ". . . l'éternité est un fruit dont le temps présent sera la fleur. Sans le don
    de l'été radieux qui descend du ciel, point du maturation à l'automne, mais
    il n'en reste pas moins que le fruit mûr se nouait et s'élaborait dans la
    floraison du printemps" (Malevez, *Bijdragen*, 10 [1949], 232).

93 Ibid., pp. 233 ff.

94 Pierre Teilhard de Chardin, *The Phenomenon of Man* (New York: Harper
    and Row, 1961); *The Divine Milieu* (New York: Harper and Brothers,
    1960).

95 M. I. Montuclard, "La Médiation de l'Eglise et la médiation de l'histoire,"
    Jeunesse de l'Eglise, 7 (1947), 9 ff.

96 J. Daniélou, *Essai sur la mystère de l'histoire* (Paris: Editions du Seuil,
    1953), p. 23.

97 "Un maître fait travailler un élève sur un ensemble de problèmes très
    difficiles. L'élève ne trouvera pas la solution, bien qu'il en approche plus
    ou moins et multiplie pour cela les essais. Cette solution lui sera donnée
    par le maître, mais seulement quand, s'étant exercé sur elle, il aura
    développé son esprit, ses puissances, d'une manière qu'il n'aurait même
    pas soupçonné si la solution lui avait été donné tout de suite. Le disciple
    se sera de quelque manière mis de niveau avec la solution; il ne la *recevra*
    vraiment que, parce que dans son effort vers elle, il se sera comme dilaté
    à sa mesure" (Yves Congar, "Pour Une Théologie du laïcat," *Etudes*, 256
    [1948], 214).

CHAPTER IV

1 As quoted by Stern, editor, *The Varieties of History*, p. 210.

2 Ibid., pp. 121 ff.

3 Ibid., pp. 126 ff.

4 Heinrich von Sybel, "Vorwort," *Historische Zeitschrift*, 1 (1859), iii.

5 As quoted by Gilbert J. Garraghan, S.J., *A Guide to Historical Method*
   (second edition by Jean Delanglez; New York: Fordham University Press,
   1946), p. 37.

6 Stern, editor, *The Varieties of History*, pp. 230 ff.

7 Ibid., p. 239.

8 For an introduction to Vico see *Oeuvres choisies*, edited by J. Chaix-Ruy
   (Paris: Presses Universitaires de France, 1946).

9   See p. 126, n. 6, in this book concerning the term *human studies.*

10   Heinrich Rickert, *Die Grenzen der naturwissenschaftlichen Begriffsbildung*
     (Tübingen: Mohr, 1929); *Kulturwissenschaft und Naturwissenschaft* (Tü-
     bingen: Mohr, 1926); *Die Probleme der Geschichtsphilosophie* (Heidelberg:
     Winter, 1924).

11   Rickert, *Die Probleme der Geschichtsphilosophie*, p. 27.

12   Rickert, *Kulturwissenschaft und Naturwissenschaft*, pp. 78 ff.

13   Rickert, *Die Probleme der Geschichtsphilosophie*, pp. 39 ff.

14   Gusdorf, *Introduction aux sciences humaines* (Paris: Les Belles Lettres,
     1960), pp. 7 ff.

15   Rickert, *Die Probleme der Geschichtsphilosophie*, pp. 32 ff.

16   Jacques Maritain, *On the Philosophy of History* (New York: Charles Scrib-
     ner's Sons, 1957), pp. 2 ff.

17   Jacques Barzun and H. F. Graff, *The Modern Researcher* (New York: Har-
     court, Brace and Company, 1957), pp. 196 ff. See also n. 19.

18   Ibid.

19   Garraghan, *A Guide to Historical Method*; William Leo Lucey, S.J., *History:
     Methods and Interpretation* (Chicago: Loyola University Press, 1958);
     Renier, *History: Its Purpose and Method*; A. von Brandt, *Werkzeug des
     Historikers* (Stuttgart: Kohlhammer, 1958). See also Select Bibliography.

20   As quoted by Stern, editor, *The Varieties of History*, p. 229. On the danger
     of overspecialization in American historiography see Barzun and Graff,
     The Modern Researcher.

21   Marrou, *De la Connaissance historique*, p. 46.

22   As quoted by Pieter Geyl, *Use and Abuse of History* (New Haven: Yale
     University Press, 1955), p. 62.

23   D'Arcy, *The Meaning and Matter of History*, p. 24.

24   Ibid., p. 22.

25   Huizinga, *Verzamelde werken*, VII, 186 ff.

26   See Wagner, *Geschichtswissenschaft*, pp. 237 ff.

27   Leopold von Ranke, *Geschichte der romanischen und germanischen Völker
     von 1494 bis 1514* (Leipzig: Duncker und Humblot, 1874), p. vii. More about
     Von Ranke's views in Wagner, *Geschichtswissenschaft*, pp. 191 ff.

28   Von Ranke, "Vorwort," *Weltgeschichte* (Leipzig: Duncker und Humblot,
     1888), IX, ix.

29   Rickert, *Die Grenzen der naturwissenschaftlichen Begriffsbildung*, pp. 357
     ff.; *Die Probleme des Geschichtsphilosophie*, p. 58.

30   L. Rogier, "Over het verkrijgen van zekerheid in de geesteswetenschappen,"
     *Verslag van de plechtige viering van het honderdvijftigjarig bestaan der
     Koninklijke Nederlandse Akademie van wetenschappen* (Amsterdam: North-
     Holland Publishing Company, 1958), pp. 120 ff.

31   See M. C. Smit, *Het goddelijk geheim in de geschiedenis* (Kampen: Kok,
     1955).

32   Romein, *Journal of the History of Ideas*, 9 (1948), 55. See also p. 8
     of this book.

33   Romein, *In de hof der historie*, p. 101.

34   Ibid., pp. 101 ff.

35 ". . . tu n'est pas le bon Dieu, n'oublie pas que tu n'est qu'un homme" (Marrou, *De la Connaissance historique*, pp. 59 ff.).

36 ". . . history, I suppose, is the Past—so far as we know it" (V. H. Galbraith, as quoted by Renier, *History: Its Purpose and Method*, p. 82).

37 Marrou, *De la Connaissance historique*, pp. 59 ff.

38 Litt, *Wissenschaft, Bildung, Weltanschauung* (Leipzig: Teubner, 1928), pp. 124 ff.

39 Geyl, *Use and Abuse of History*, pp. 63 ff.

40 Ibid., p. 71.

41 Ibid., p. 51.

42 See p. 3 of this book.

43 Eric Dardel, *L'Histoire, science du concret* (Paris: Presses Universitaires de France, 1946), pp. 10 ff.

44 Renier, *History: Its Purpose and Method*, p. 159.

45 Max Scheler, *On the Eternal in Man*, translated by Bernard Noble (New York: Harper and Row, 1961).

46 Rogier, *Verslag van de plechtige viering*, p. 127.

47 Marrou, *De la Connaissance historique*, pp. 98 ff.

48 Voggensperger, *Der Begriff der Geschichte*, p. 85.

49 "Hier ist zu beachten, dass der Historiker sichselbst nie vergessen kann, dass er zum universalen historischen Horizont, in den er hineinforscht, thematisch mitgehört. Er selbst als Person ist Mitglied des universalen geschichtlichen Seins. Sein Weltleben ist Moment des universalen geschichtlichen Menschheitslebens, das sein universales Thema ist. Wie eng [*changed to* weit] er auch sein spezielles Arbeitsthema [auch] begrenzen mag, auch von dem ist et thematisch nicht völlig ablösbar. *Jede Erfahrung, jede begrenzende Festellung*, die ich im Leben über Andere mache, *mache ich notwendig von mir aus*. Andere sind für mich Andere von mir aus, sie sind aus meiner Erfahrung für mich seiend und soseiend . . . Ich bin immer als Ich mit dabei . . . Eine Geschichte, die endgültig [*in margin* überzeitlich] feststellen könnte, 'wie es eigentlich gewesen ist,' ist aus prinzipiellen Gründen eine Unmöglichkeit. Das methodische Ideal des Historikers an einer Wahrheitsidee orientieren zu wollen, die prinzipiell [*changed in margin to* im Wesen] dieselbe sei wie in den exakten Wissenschaften, das heisse, einem widersinnigen Ziele nachjagen" (E. Husserl, "Zur Geschichtsphilosophie," manuscript [Louvain: Husserlarchives, 1936], M III 5 III 4 a, b).

50 Henri Sérouya, *Spinoza* (Paris: Albin Michel, 1947), p. 23.

51 Barzun and Graff, *The Modern Researcher*, pp. 187 ff.

52 "La connaissance d'une personne spirituelle n'est pas discursive: une conscience ne se construit pas du dehors; une personne ne s'atteint pas au terme d'une série de relations abstraites. La fonction discursive de l'intelligence peut bien préparer, mais non accomplir cette saisie d'une existence concrète. Elle ne peut pas réaliser ce phénomène d'interpretation en bloc qu'est la découverte d'une personne semblable à moi; et elle peut moins encore pénétrer au secret de cette personne spirituelle unique et fraternelle tout ensemble. A supposer que le 'noyau spirituel' de l'être puisse se révéler

à un autre, comme le voulait M. Scheler, reste que ce sera sur un plan non discursif: existence et valeur de la personne échappent à cette fonction de l'intelligence, elles sont 'obscures' pour elle. De plus, il faut reconnaître que cette perception n'est pas pénétration lumineuse d'un dedans. Elle est beaucoup plus la saisie globale d'une existence spirituelle, une sorte de *contact* et de *coïncidence* avec l'être découvert—susceptibles l'un et l'autre d'un approfondissement indéfini, mais en partie opaques et résistants à la raison. Or c'est là que se situe l'acte de foi et, par suite, il se place de lui-même sur un plan obscur et irritant pour la pure raison: l'univers des personnes est un monde où l'on n'entre vraiment que par l'amour" (Jean Mouroux, "Je crois en toi," *Revue des Jeunes*, 1949, pp. 55 ff.).

53 See also Nota, *Max Scheler* (Utrecht: Spectrum, 1947), pp. 170 ff., for a reference to some passages in Aquinas and a list of other related works. A clear exposition of Newman's views is to be found in A. J. Boekraad, *The Personal Conquest of Truth According to J. H. Newman* (Louvain: Editions E. Nauwelaerts, 1955).

SELECT BIBLIOGRAPHY

Works by such "classic" authors on the subject of this work as Plato, St. Augustine, St. Thomas Aquinas, Hegel, Marx, and Von Ranke have not been included unless they are available in recent, inexpensive editions which might be helpful to new readers. Contemporary authors are listed only when they deal explicitly with the theme.

History and Theory: Studies in the Philosophy of History, published periodically by Mouton and Company, The Hague, concentrates primarily on the subject of the theory of history. A bibliography covering the years 1945-1957 is to be found in Volume I (1961).

135

For an analytical bibliography see J. Watkins, "Philosophy of History," and Henri I. Marrou, "Philosophie de l'histoire," in *Philosophy in the Mid-century*, edited by Raymond Klibansky (Florence: La Nuova Italia, 1958), pp. 158 ff.

Adams, A. *Transzendenz der Erkenntnis und Eschatologie der Geschichte.* Münster: Aschendorf, 1958.

Ariès, P. *Le Temps de l'histoire.* Monaco: Du Rocher, 1954.

Aron, R. *Introduction à la philosophie de l'histoire.* Paris: Gallimard, 1948.

Barzun, Jacques, and H. F. Graff. *The Modern Researcher.* New York: Harcourt, Brace and Company, 1957.

Bauhofer, O. *Das Geheimnis der Zeiten: Christliche Sinndeutung der Geschichte.* Munich: Kösel und Pustet, 1935.

Beauvoir, Simone de. *Tous les Hommes sont mortels.* Paris: Gallimard, 1946.

Bellon, K. *Wijsbegeerte der geschiedenis.* Antwerp: Philosophische Bibliotheek Standaardboekhandel, 1953.

Berkhof, H. *Christus, der zin der geschiedenis.* Nijkerk: Callenbach, 1958.

Bloch, Marc. *Apologie pour l'histoire ou métier d'historien.* Paris: Colin, 1949. Translated from the French by Peter Putnam as *The Historian's Craft.* Manchester: Manchester University Press, 1954.

Brandt, A. von. *Werkzeug des Historikers.* Stuttgart: Kohlhammer, 1958.

Breysig, K. *Gesellschaftslehre, Geschichtslehre.* Berlin: Walter de Gruyter, 1958.

Brüning, W. *Geschichtsphilosophie der Gegenwart.* Stuttgart: Klett, 1961.

Brunner, A. *Geschichtlichkeit.* Bern: Francke, 1961.

Bultmann, Rudolf. *History and Eschatology.* New York: Harper and Row, 1962.

Burckhardt, J. *Weltgeschichtliche Betrachtungen.* Stuttgart: Kröner, 1955, reprint.

Butterfield, Herbert. *Christianity and History.* New York: Charles Scribner's Sons, 1960.

Cairns, Grace. *Philosophies of History.* Foreword by Pitirim A. Sorokin. New York: Philosophical Library, 1962.

Carr, Edward H. *What Is History?* New York: Alfred A. Knopf, 1962.

Chaix-Ruy, J. *St. Augustin: Temps et histoire.* Paris: Etudes Augustiniennes, 1956.

Chenu, M. D. "Conscience de l'histoire et théologie au douzième siècle," *Archives d'histoire doctrinale et littéraire du Moyen Age*, 107 ff.

Christentum und Geschichte: Vorträge der Tagung in Bochum. Edited by Vorstand des Landesverbandes nordhein-westfälischer Geschichtslehrer. October 5-8, 1954. Düsseldorf: Schwann, 1955.

Collingwood, R. G. *The Idea of History.* Edited by T. M. Knox. Oxford: Oxford University Press, 1946.

Connolly, James M. *Human History and the Word of God.* New York: The Macmillan Company, 1965.

Copleston, Frederick. *A History of Philosophy.* Vol. VI: *The Rise of the Philosophy of History.* Garden City: Doubleday and Company, 1964. Pp. 173 ff.

Cox, D. *History and Myth.* London: Darton, Longman and Todd, 1961.

Croce, B. *Die Geschichte als Gedanke und als Tat.* Bern: Francke, 1944.

Cullmann, Oscar. *Christ and Time: The Primitive Conception of Time and History.* Translated from the German by Floyd F. Filson. Revised edition. Philadelphia: Westminster Press, 1964.

Danièlou, J. *Essai sur le mystère de l'histoire.* Paris: Editions du Seuil, 1953.

Danto, Arthur C. *Analytical Philosophy of History*. Cambridge: Cambridge University Press, 1965.

D'Arcy, M. C. *The Meaning and Matter of History: A Christian View*. New York: Meridian Books, 1961.

Dardel, Eric. *L'Histoire, science du concret*. Paris: Presses Universitaires de France, 1946.

Dawson, Christopher. *The Historic Reality of Christian Culture*. New York: Harper and Brothers, 1960.

———— *Progress and Religion*. Garden City: Doubleday and Company, 1945.

Delfgaauw, Bernard. *Geschiedenis en vooruitgang*. Baarn: Wereldvenster, 1961-1964. Vols. I-III.

Dempf, A. *Die Krisis des Fortschrittsglaubens*. Vienna: Herder, 1947.

Dilthey, Wilhelm. *Einleitung in die Geisteswissenschaften*. Leipzig: Teubner, 1923. Vol. I.

Dondeyne, Albert. *Contemporary European Thought and Christian Faith*. Pittsburgh: Duquesne University Press, 1958.

Dray, William H. *Philosophy of History*. Englewood Cliffs: Prentice-Hall, 1964.

Eliade, Mircea. *Cosmos and History: The Myth of the Eternal Return*. New York: Harper and Brothers, 1959.

Ellman, Richard, and C. Feidelson, Jr. *The Modern Tradition*. New York: Oxford University Press, 1965.

Féret, H. *L'Apocalypse de S. Jean: Vision chrétienne de l'histoire*. Paris: Corrêa, 1946.

Fessard, G. "Attitude ambivalente de Hegel en face de l'histoire," *Archives de Philosophie*, XXIV (1961), 207 ff.

———— *De l'Actualité historique*. Bruges: Desclée de Brouwer, 1960. Vols. I-II.

Fiore, Joachim of. *Das Reich des heiligen Geistes*. Bearbeitung Alfons Rosenberg. Munich: Barth, 1954.

Frankfort, Henri, and others. *Before Philosophy*. London: Penguin Books, 1959.

Fueter, E. *Geschichte, der neueren Historiographie.* Munich: Oldenbourg, 1936.

Gallie, W. B. *Philosophy and the Historical Understanding.* New York: Schocken Books, 1964.

Gardiner, Patrick. *The Nature of Historical Explanation.* London: Oxford University Press, 1952.

———, editor. *Theories of History.* New York: The Free Press of Glencoe, 1958.

Gargan, Edward T., editor. *The Intent of Toynbee's History.* Chicago: Loyola University Press, 1961.

Garraghan, Gilbert J., S.J. *A Guide to Historical Method.* Second edition by Jean Delanglez. New York: Fordham University Press, 1946.

Geyl, Pieter. *Debates with Historians.* New York: Meridian Books, 1958.

——— *Use and Abuse of History.* New Haven: Yale University Press, 1955.

Gouhier, H. *L'Histoire et sa philosophie.* Paris: Vrin, 1952.

Groningen, B. A. van. *In the Grip of the Past: Essay on an Aspect of Greek Thought.* "Philosophia Antiqua," Vol. VI. Leiden: E. J. Brill, 1953.

Gusdorf, G. *Introduction aux sciences humaines.* Paris: Les Belles Lettres, 1960.

——— *Mythe et métaphysique.* Paris: Flammarion, 1953.

Gutzwiller, R. *Herr der Herrscher: Christus in der geheimen Offenbarung.* Einsiedeln: Benziger, 1951.

Haecker, T. *Der Christ und die Geschichte.* Munich: Kösel, 1949.

Heidegger, Martin. *Sein und Zeit.* Halle: Max Niemeyer, 1941. Translated as *Being and Time* by John Macquarrie and Edward Robinson. New York: Harper and Row, 1962.

Heimsoeth, H. *Geschichtsphilosophie.* Bonn: Bouvier, 1949.

Herder, J. G. *Zur Philosophie der Geschichte.* Auswahl von W. Harich. Berlin: Aufbau Verlag, 1952. Vols. I-II.

Hodges, Herbert A. *Wilhelm Dilthey: An Introduction*. London: Kegan Paul, Trench, Trubner and Company, 1944.

Hofer, W. *Geschichte zwischen Philosophie und Politik*. Basel: Verlag für Recht und Gesellschaft, 1956.

Holm, S. *Søren Kierkegaards Geschichtsphilosophie*. Stuttgart: Kohlhammer, 1956.

L'Homme et l'histoire: Actes du sixième congrès des sociétés de philosophie en langue française. Paris: Presses Universitaires de France, 1952.

Hook, Sydney, editor. *Philosophy and History: A Symposium*. New York: New York University, 1963.

Huizinga, Johan. *Verzamelde werken*. Vol. VII: *Geschiedwetenschap, Hedendaagse cultuur*. Haarlem: H. D. Tjeenk Willink en Zoon, 1948-1953. Pp. 35-94 translated in *Men and Ideas*, pp. 17-76. New York: Meridian Books, 1959. Pp. 134-50 translated in Fritz Stern, editor. *The Varieties of History: From Voltaire to the Present*, pp. 289-303. New York: Meridian Books, 1956.

Jaspers, Karl. *The Origin and Goal of History*. Translated from the German by Michael Bullock. New Haven: Yale University Press, 1953.

Klibansky, Raymond, and H. J. Paton, editors. *Philosophy and History: The Ernst Cassirer Festschrift*. New York: Harper and Row, 1963.

Krüger, G. *Freiheit und Weltverwaltung: Aufsätze zur Philosophie der Geschichte*. Freiburg: Alber, 1958.

——— *Grundfragen der Philosophie: Geschichte, Wahrheit, Wissenschaft*. Frankfurt: Klostermann, 1958.

Kuypers, K. *Theorie der geschiedenis*. Amsterdam: H. Paris, 1931.

Lacroix, J., and J. Nélis. *Culture et civilisation: Initiation à l'humanisme historique*. Tournai: Casterman, 1957.

Langeveld, M. "Psychology and Physiology of Man," in *Verkenning en verdieping*. Purmerend: Muuses, 1950. Pp. 147 ff.

Laslowski, E. *Geschichte aus dem Glauben.* Freiburg: Herder and Company, 1949.

Lauffer, Siegfried. "Der antike Fortschrittsgedanke," in *Proceedings of the Eleventh International Congress of Philosophy*, Brussels, August 20-26, 1953. Amsterdam: North-Holland Publishing Company; Louvain: Editions E. Nauwelaerts, 1953. XII, 37 ff.

Lewis, H. D. *Freedom and History.* New York: The Macmillan Company, 1962.

Litt, T. *Das Allgemeine im Aufbau der geisteswissenschaftlichen Erkenntnis.* Leipzig: Hirzel, 1941.

———— *Geschichtswissenschaft und Geschichtsphilosophie.* Munich: Bruckmann, 1950.

———— *Wege und Irrwege geschichtlichen Denkens.* Munich: Piper and Company, 1948.

———— *Die Wiedererweckung des geschichtlichen Bewusstseins.* Heidelberg: Quelle und Meyer, 1956.

Löwith, Karl. *Gesammelte Abhandlungen: Zur Kritik der geschichtlichen Existenz.* Stuttgart: Kohlhammer, 1960.

———— *Meaning in History: The Theological Implications of the Philosophy of History.* Chicago: University of Chicago Press, 1949.

Lucey, William Leo, S.J. *History: Methods and Interpretation.* Chicago: Loyola University Press, 1958.

Malevez, L. "Deux Théologies catholiques de l'histoire," *Bijdragen der Nederlandse Jezuieten*, 10 (1949), 225 ff.

———— "La Vision chrétienne de l'histoire," *Nouvelle Revue Théologique*, 71 (1949), 113 ff., 244 ff.

Maritain, Jacques. *On the Philosophy of History.* New York: Charles Scribner's Sons, 1957.

Marrou, Henri I. *L'Ambivalence du temps de l'histoire chez S. Augustin.* Paris: Vrin, 1950.

Marrou, Henri I. *De la Connaissance historique*. Paris: Editions du Seuil, 1954. Translated as *The Meaning of History*. Baltimore: Helicon Press, 1966.

———— "Philosophie critique de l'histoire et 'sens de l'histoire,' " in *L'Homme et l'histoire: Actes du sixième congrès des sociétés de philosophie en langue française*. Paris: Presses Universitaires de France, 1952. Pp. 3 ff.

Meinecke, F. *Vom geschichtlichen Sinn und vom Sinn der Geschichte*. Leipzig: Köhler und Amelang, 1939.

Mensch und Zeit: Eranos-Jahrbuch. Zurich: Rhein-Verlag, 1952. Vol. 20 (1951).

Merleau-Ponty, M. *Les Sciences de l'homme et la phénoménologie*. Paris: Les cours de Sorbonne, Centre de documentation universitaire, n. d.

Meyerhoff, Hans, editor. *The Philosophy of History in Our Time*. Garden City: Doubleday and Company, 1959.

Mouroux, Jean. *The Mystery of Time: A Theological Inquiry*. Translated by John Drury. New York: Desclee Company, 1964.

Müller, M. *Expérience et histoire*. Louvain: Université de Louvain, 1959.

Niebuhr, Reinhold. *Faith and History*. New York: Charles Scribner's Sons, 1949.

Nota, J. H., S.J. *Max Scheler*. Utrecht: Spectrum, 1947.

———— "Le Point de départ de la philosophie de l'histoire," in *Proceedings of the Eleventh International Congress of Philosophy*, Brussels, August 20-26, 1953. Amsterdam: North-Holland Publishing Company; Louvain: Editions E. Nauwelaerts, 1953.

Ortega y Gasset, José. *Obras Completas*. Vol. IV: *La "Filosofía de la Historia" de Hegel y la Historiología*. Madrid: Revista de Occidente, 1957.

Pearsen, C. V. "Le Sens du temps historique," in *L'Homme et l'histoire: Actes du sixième congrès des sociétés de philoso-*

phie en langue française. Paris: Presses Universitaires de France, 1952.

Philosophie de l'histoire. Vol. VIII, *Proceedings of the Eleventh International Congress of Philosophy*, Brussels, August 20-26, 1953. Amsterdam: North-Holland Publishing Company; Louvain: Editions E. Nauwelaerts, 1953.

Philosophies de l'histoire: Recherches et débats, 17 (October 1956).

Pieper, Josef. *The End of Time: A Meditation on the Philosophy of History*. Translated by Michael Bullock. New York: Pantheon Books, 1954.

Polak, F. *Hoopvolle toekomstperspectieven*. Utrecht: W. de Haan, 1957.

—————*De toekomst is verleden tijd*. Utrecht: W. de Haan, 1957. Vols. I-II.

Pos, H. *Keur uit de verspreide geschriften*. Vol. II: *Beginselen en gestalten*. Arnhem: Van Loghum Slaterus, Van Gorcum, 1958.

Pot, J. van der. "De filosofie der geschiedenis," in *Scientia*. Zeist: De Haan, 1956, I, 307 ff.

—————*De periodisering der geschiedenis*. Met een voorwoord van J. Romein. The Hague: Van Stockum, 1951.

—————"Theorie of filosophie der geschiedenis?" *Tijdschrift voor geschiedenis*, LXX (1957), 377 ff.

Puech, H. C. "Temps, histoire et mythe dans le christianisme des premiers siècles," in *Proceedings of the Seventh Congress of History of Religions*. Amsterdam: North-Holland Publishing Company, 1951. Pp. 33 ff.

Ranke, Leopold von. *Ueber die Epochen der neueren Geschichte*. Laupheim: Steiner, 1948.

Renier, G. J. *History: Its Purpose and Method*. Boston: Beacon Press, 1950.

Richardson, Alan. *History, Sacred and Profane*. Philadelphia: The Westminster Press, 1964.

Rickert, Heinrich. *Die Grenzen der naturwissenschaftlichen Begriffsbildung.* Tübingen: Mohr, 1929.

———— *Kulturwissenschaft und Naturwissenschaft.* Tübingen: Mohr, 1926.

———— *Die Probleme der Geschichtsphilosophie.* Heidelberg: Winter, 1924.

Ritter, G. *Geschichte als Bildungsmacht.* Stuttgart: Deutsche Verlags-Anstalt, 1947.

Robbers, H. "Heeft het infra-humane geschiedenis?" *Tijdschrift voor Philosophie*, XVI (1954), 37 ff.

Rogier, L. "Over het verkrijgen van zekerheid in de geesteswetenschappen," *Verslag van de plechtige viering van het honderdvijftigjarig bestaan der Koninklijke Nederlandse Akademie van wetenschappen.* Amsterdam: North-Holland Publishing Company, 1958. Pp. 116 ff.

————, editor. *De zin der geschiedenis voor geloof en rede.* Heerlen: Winants, n. d.

Romein, Jan. *Carillon der tijden.* Amsterdam: Querido, 1953.

———— *Eender en anders.* Amsterdam: Querido, 1964.

———— *Het onvoltooid verleden.* Amsterdam: Querido, 1948.

———— *In de hof der historie.* Amsterdam: Querido, 1951.

———— "Theoretical History," *Journal of the History of Ideas*, 9 (1948), 53 ff.

———— *Tussen vrees en vrijheid.* Amsterdam: Querido, 1950.

Rossmann, K. *Deutsche Geschichtsphilosophie von Lessing bis Jaspers.* Bremen: Schünemann, 1959.

Rothacker, E. *Logik und Systematik der Geisteswissenschaften.* Bonn: Bouvier, 1948.

Sartre, Jean-Paul. *Critique de la raison dialectique.* Paris: Gallimard, 1960.

Scheler, Max. *Philosophical Perspectives.* Boston: Beacon Press, 1958.

Schilfgaarde, P. van. *De zin der geschiedenis.* Leiden: Brill, 1946-1947. Vols. I-III.

144

Seypel, J. *Dekadenz oder Fortschritt: Eine Studie Amerikanischer Geschichtsphilosophie.* Schlehdorf: Bronnen-Verlag, 1951.

Smit, M. C. *De verhouding van Christendom en historie in de huidige rooms-katholieke geschiedbeschouwing.* Kampen: Kok, 1950.

Smith, Page. *The Historian and History.* New York: Alfred A. Knopf, 1964.

Spiess, E. *Die Grundfragen der Geschichtsphilosophie.* Schwyz: Verlagsbuchh Maria Hilf, 1937.

Stambauch, J. *Untersuchungen zum Problem der Zeit bei Nietzsche.* The Hague: Nijhoff, 1959.

Stern, Alfred. *Philosophy of History and the Problem of Values.* The Hague: Humanities Press, 1962.

Stern, Fritz, editor. *The Varieties of History: From Voltaire to the Present.* New York: Meridian Books, 1956.

Stucki, P. A. *Le Christianisme et l'histoire d'après Kierkegaard.* Basel: Verlag für Recht und Gesellschaft, 1963.

Teilhard de Chardin, Pierre. *The Phenomenon of Man.* New York: Harper and Row, 1961.

Thieme, K. *Gott und die Geschichte.* Freiburg: Herder and Company, 1948.

Thils, G. *Théologie des réalitiés terrestres.* Paris: Desclée de Brouwer, 1947-1949.

Thyssen, J. *Geschichte des Geschichtsphilosophie.* Bonn: Bouvier, 1954.

Toynbee, Alfred. *A Study of History.* New York: Oxford University Press, 1934-1961. Vols. I-XII.

Urs von Balthasar, H. *Das Ganze im Fragment.* Einsiedeln: Benziger, 1963.

———— *A Theology of History.* New York: Sheed and Ward, 1963.

Vico, Giovanni Battista. *Oeuvres choisies.* Edited by J. Chaix-Ruy. Paris: Presses Universitaires de France, 1946.

Voegelin, Eric. *Order and History*. Baton Rouge: Louisiana State University Press, 1956-1957. Vols. I-III.

Voggensperger, R. *Der Begriff der Geschichte als Wissenschaft im Lichte aristotelisch-thomistischer Prinzipien*. Freiburg: Paulus-Verlag, 1948.

Waelhens, A. de. "Sciences humaines, horizon ontologique et rencontre," in *Existence et signification*. Louvain: Editions E. Nauwelaerts, 1958. Pp. 233 ff.

Wagner, Fritz. *Geschichtswissenschaft*. Freiburg: Alber, 1951.

—————— *Moderne Geschichtsschreibung*. Berlin: Duncker und Humblot, 1960.

Walsh, W. H. *Philosophy of History*. New York: Harper and Brothers, 1960.

Weber, A. *Prinzipien der Geschichts- und Kultur-soziologie*. Munich: Piper and Company, 1951.

Weill, R. *Aristote et l'histoire: Essais sur la politique*. Paris: Klincksieck, 1960.

Weiss, Paul. *History: Written and Lived*. Carbondale: Southern Illinois University Press, 1962.

INDEX OF NAMES

147

About this book

Phenomenology and History was designed by William Nicoll of Edit, Inc. It was set in the composing room of Loyola University Press. The text is 12 on 14 Bodoni Book; the reduced matter, 10 on 12; the notes, 8 on 10. The display type is 12 Bodoni Book caps.

It was printed by Photopress, Inc., on Warren's 60-pound English Finish paper and bound by A. C. Engdahl and Company, Inc., in Bancroft cloth.